HAUNTED MERIDIAN, MISSISSIPPI

HAUNTED MERIDIAN, MISSISSIPPI

ALAN BROWN

Haunted America

Published by Haunted America
A Division of The History Press
Charleston, SC 29403
www.historypress.net

First published 2011

Manufactured in the United States

ISBN 978.1.60949.123.9

Library of Congress Cataloging-in-Publication Data

Brown, Alan, 1950 Jan. 12-
Haunted Meridian, Mississippi / Alan Brown.
p. cm.
Includes bibliographical references (p.).
ISBN 978-1-60949-123-9
1. Ghosts--Mississippi--Meridian. I. Title.
BF1472.U6B74275 2011
133.109762'676--dc23
2011026263

Notice: The information in this book is true and complete to the best of our knowledge. It is offered without guarantee on the part of the author or The History Press. The author and The History Press disclaim all liability in connection with the use of this book.

To Cade Walker, in the hope that he will love reading as much as his father and grandfather do.

CONTENTS

Contents

ACKNOWLEDGEMENTS

Because much of the material in this book was provided through personal interviews, I am indebted to a number of individuals. Deputy Sheriff Ward Calhoun III introduced me to a number of "talkative" people in the Lauderdale County Courthouse, like Stanley Shannon, who took me on a tour of the old building. Ward Calhoun Jr., director of the Lauderdale County Department of Archives and History, graciously shared his time and knowledge of Lauderdale County with me. Joel Seltmann, my neighbor, helped me gain access to Hooper's Electronics. Radio personalities Scotty Ray Boyd and Debbie Alexander not only accompanied me on my visits to haunted sites but also publicized our adventures on the air. *Meridian Star* reporter Jennifer Jacobs Brown, *Meridian Star* photographer Paula Merritt and local librarian Kevin Chathom also assisted me during investigations of Meridian's haunted places. The information Jim McRae and Greg Hatcher gave me really enhanced my chapter on the Soulé Steam Feed Works. My father-in-law, Paul Quick, assisted me with photography. My greatest source of information was Fonda Rush, whose stories about the ghosts of Meridian inspired me to write the book. However, *Haunted Meridian, Mississippi* would never have been written if my wife, Marilyn, and my daughters, Andrea and Vanessa, had not encouraged me to seek out a publisher.

INTRODUCTION

Meridian, Mississippi, has experienced more than its share of highs and lows over the years. Like many towns and cities in Mississippi and Alabama, Meridian's history began in 1831. In 1830, the Choctaws sold the land to the United States. The first settler in Meridian was a transplanted native of Virginia named Richard McLemore, who received a federal land grant of two thousand acres. McLemore attempted to lure more people to the area with the offer of free land. Meridian became a genuine town after 1853, following construction of the Mobile & Ohio Railroad. Thanks to an influx of railroad workers and their families, Meridian was officially incorporated on January 10, 1860. During the Civil War, Meridian was the site of a Confederate hospital, an arsenal, a prisoner-of-war stockade and a number of state offices. The newly incorporated town suffered a serious setback on February 14, 1864, when General William Tecumseh Sherman and the Union army raided Meridian, burning the gristmills and destroying the railroad tracks. Meridian rebounded after the fall of the Confederacy in April 1865.

The railroads were rebuilt and operating after only twenty-six days. Stores, banks and factories were built as well. However, the 1870s proved to be a turbulent decade for the people of Meridian. During the Meridian Race Riot of 1871, the entire downtown area was destroyed by fire. Serious economic problems plagued the city during the Panic of 1873. The yellow fever epidemic of 1878 exacerbated the city's difficulties, claiming eighty-six victims.

The next several decades proved to be a time of healing and growth for the embittered city. In the 1880s, electricity and running water were installed in many homes and public buildings. Streets and sidewalks were paved, and a sewage system was created. The timber and cotton that passed into and out of Meridian on the railroad initiated the city's Progressive era between 1890 and 1930. Factories like the Southern Oil and Fertilizer Company earned Meridian the reputation as one of the South's leading manufacturing centers. It was also during this time that two of the city's most impressive structures—the Grand Opera House (1890) and the Threefoot Building—were constructed.

Meridian changed with the times over the next seventy years, but change did not come easily. Its downtown section began to wane after World War II. The city also suffered in the 1950s with gradual erosion of the importance of the railroad in the South. In the 1960s, tension between blacks and whites occasionally erupted in violence.

Today, the scars of the past are barely visible. Military conflict and racial strife are, for the most part, relics of the past. Meridian is known worldwide for the speakers and amplifiers produced by Peavey Electronics. A number of celebrities also hail from Meridian, such as Jimmie Rodgers, the "Father of Country Music"; aviation pioneers the Key brothers; and actress Sela Ward.

My purpose in writing this book is to cement Meridian's reputation as one of the most haunted cities in the entire South. After you read *Haunted Meridian*, I hope you will agree with me that Meridian, Mississippi, is much more than just an old railroad town.

Stuckey's Bridge

In the South, haunted bridges are almost as common as haunted houses. Sometimes, bridges are haunted by the ghosts of drivers who never quite made it across. A case in point is an old iron bridge in Boyd, Alabama. Around the turn of the twentieth century, a young couple who had just gotten married in a nearby church was driving a buggy across the bridge when a rattlesnake spooked the horse, causing the buggy and its occupants to plunge into the Sucarnochee River. The screams of the unfortunate bride and groom can still be heard on the anniversary of their deaths.

In states like Alabama, Georgia and Mississippi, most haunted bridges can be classified as "Cry Baby Bridges." The story goes that one moonlit night, an unmarried woman walks onto the middle of the bridge with a baby in her arms. She climbs up on the railing and jumps into the river. The cries of the drowned baby can still be heard on nights when the moon is full. In Lauderdale County, near the little town of Chunky, the best-known haunted bridge is Stuckey's Bridge.

Stuckey's Bridge, the oldest iron bridge in Lauderdale County, is located approximately twelve miles southwest of downtown Meridian. When it was built in 1851, the bridge was situated on the main route across the Chunky River. The bridge was rebuilt in 1901 by the Virginia Bridge and Iron Company. On August 4, 1984, Stuckey's Bridge was listed as a Mississippi Landmark. Four years later, on November 16, 1988, Stuckey's Bridge was added to the National Register of Historic Places. The decking of the old bridge was replaced in 2001. A few years later, the board of supervisors

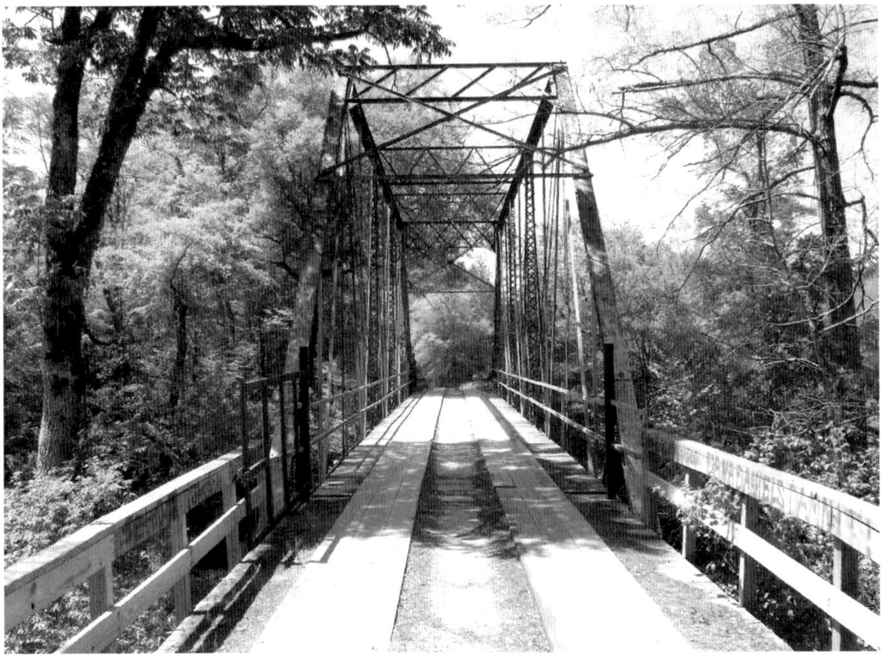

Stuckey's Bridge.

closed Stuckey's Bridge to vehicular traffic because it had become structurally unsound. The closing of Stuckey's Bridge has not even slowed down the steady stream of teenagers and curiosity-seekers who drive down Stuckey's Bridge Road every year in the hope of catching a glimpse of the ghosts that haunt Stuckey's Bridge.

According to legend, sometime after the Civil War, a man named Stuckey owned an inn not far from Stuckey's Bridge along a stage route. Some say he was a member of the Dalton gang. After the sun went down, Stuckey stood in the middle of the bridge with a lantern in hand and signaled to flatboats and rafts loaded with produce and cotton on their way to the markets in Meridian. Approximately twenty men, weary from the long trip down the Chunky River, took Stuckey up on his offer of a hot meal and a soft bed. Sometime during the night, Stuckey snuck into his guests' bedroom and knocked them on the head. He then buried their bodies somewhere around the bridge and confiscated their goods. Rumors of the disappearances at Stuckey's Inn were brought to the attention of the local sheriff, who organized a posse. The men arrested Stuckey and hanged him from one of the trusses, not far from where he had stood with his lantern, luring his victims to the inn. The outlaw was left dangling from the bridge for five days before the rope was cut and his body dropped into the river.

Since the 1930s, people living in and around Chunky have passed down tales about the haunting of Stuckey's Bridge. People claimed to have seen an old man holding a lantern walking along the banks of the Chunky River and crossing the bridge. Witnesses bold enough to visit the bridge at night have also heard a loud splashing sound in the river under the bridge. They say that it sounded like something heavy had fallen off the bridge—like a human body. Legend has it that a strange glow appers at the spot where the splash occurs. A few people even claim to have seen Stuckey's corpse hanging from the bridge during a full moon. Young people who have parked their cars and trucks on the bridge say they have heard the screams of Stuckey's victims echoing through the night air. One group of teenagers said that they were sitting in the middle of the bridge with their truck in neutral when suddenly the truck began to move, as if someone were pushing it.

To get to Stuckey's Bridge, take the Savoy exit off I-50 South. Turn left on Meehan-Savoy Road and drive approximately two miles. Turn left on Stuckey Bridge Road. Visitors to the old bridge are allowed to walk across it, but vehicles are prohibited.

Meridian Plastic Surgery (Cahn—Crawford House)

Like Birmingham, Alabama, Meridian owes a great deal to its Jewish community. By the early 1900s, approximately one thousand Jews lived in Meridian. Jewish businessmen and entrepreneurs helped Meridian become one of the most prosperous cities in the state in the late nineteenth and early twentieth centuries. Names like Strauss, Loeb, Rosenbaum, Arkey, Threefoot, Davidson, Goldman, Lerner, Dravin and Feinstein are forever linked with the early history of the city. After the Civil War, Jewish peddlers sold their wares in the rural areas surrounding the burgeoning town. One of the first Jewish businesses in Meridian was Marks and Lichtenstein and Company, which was grossing approximately $1.5 million annually by the mid-1880s. I. Marks eventually went into business with his two half brothers, the Rothenbergs, and opened a wholesale grocery and dry goods business next to the Grand Opera House.

By the early 1900s, Jewish merchants were selling jewelry, flatware, clothing, country produce, leather goods and cotton in Meridian. The city's Jews also distinguished themselves in the legal and medical professions. In addition, they made invaluable contributions to the community. For example, the I.A. Rosenbaum family endowed the Rosenbaum Award at Meridian High School for excellence in academics and athletics.

At the turn of the nineteenth century, many of Meridian's most prominent Jewish businessmen lived on Twenty-second Avenue, which was known as "Silk Stocking Row" because of all the luxurious homes that once lined the street. One of the few remaining mansions on this street is the Cahn-Crawford House at 1200 Twenty-second Avenue. The house was built in 1918 by Edward

Cahn, who founded the Eagle Cotton Oil Company in 1894. Cahn also owned the Cahn Bank Building, which later became the Masonic Temple Building. In 1979, the house was added to the National Register of Historic Places. At the time, it was owned by Mrs. Marie Crawford.

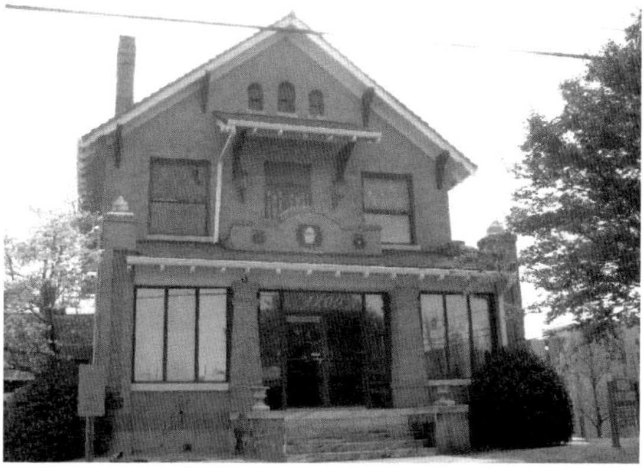

Meridian Plastic Surgery.

The beautiful old mansion is noteworthy for its majestic staircase, which ascends to a large, balconied entry portico with corner piers capped by stone finials. The striking first-floor windows are made of beveled leaded glass. Another distinctive feature of the Cahn-Crawford House is the ghost that occasionally makes an appearance.

In the 1990s, the Cahn-Crawford House was converted into Hollybrook Restaurant. In 1998, a plastic surgeon, Dr. Lee Thornton, purchased the old house. Two weeks before Meridian Plastic Surgery opened in November 1998, two waiters who had worked at Hollybrook told Dr. Thornton a strange story. "They asked me if I had met the ghost yet," Dr. Thornton said. "They said her name was Mary, and she was the ghost of a little girl who had died inside the house. I told them that nothing unusual had happened inside the old house so far."

A few weeks later, Dr. Thornton discovered that there might be some truth to the story the waiters had told him: "The man who owned the business across the street told me that the night before, he had seen a little girl standing in front of a window on the third floor. I told him that the house was completely empty when my staff and I left that afternoon."

The renovation of the Cahn-Crawford House continued during the clinic's first few months of operation. "We hired a man named Marcel to redo the floors," Dr. Thornton said.

> *He did his work after closing hours. One morning, he asked my nurse if anyone was working inside the building the night before. When she said that he was the only one in the house, he told her about hearing footsteps on third floor. From then on, he refused to work inside the house by himself. He usually brought his wife with him.*

Dr. Thornton's nurse, Lisa Marshall, has had the most encounters with Mary. "She started out as being really skeptical," Dr. Thornton said. "It wasn't long before she changed her mind about ghosts."

Lisa said that the first time she realized Mary was real, she had arrived an hour before the clinic opened and walked downstairs to clean the instruments, just as she did every morning. "While I was down there, I heard someone walking on the floor right above me," Lisa said. "I got scared because I thought there was an intruder inside the office. When I walked upstairs, though, there was no one there." She continued to hear the footsteps for several weeks in a row: "Sometimes when I was downstairs, I heard someone walking on the third floor. I could tell the footsteps were coming from the third floor because they weren't as loud."

One morning, when Lisa was in the basement, she heard an entirely different sound upstairs:

> *I was down there for just a few minutes when I heard music coming from the CD player in the waiting room. I hadn't turned it on because I didn't know how. When the receptionist came in, she heard the music, and she asked me if I had turned it on. I said no. She said someone must have because she distinctly remembered turning off the CD player the night before.*

Lisa said that Mary has made her presence known in other ways as well:

> *One morning, I opened up the double doors to the side of the nurses' station and cleaned the room. I then went downstairs. When I came back up an hour later, the doors were closed. At first, I thought Dr. Thornton was inside the room with a patient. I opened the door a crack and peeked inside. No one was there.*

Lisa recalled one occasion when Mary seemed to have expressed her displeasure. "We were really busy that day," she said. "After a while, there was this really bad smell in the house. It smelled like old tuna fish. We traced the smell to the room up in Skin Care where they put on the makeup. I think this was Mary's way of showing that she didn't like having so many strange people in her house at one time."

Except for the first morning when Lisa heard the footsteps on the floor above her, she has never really felt afraid inside the Cahn-Crawford House. "I guess I'm more afraid of real people than I am of ghosts," she said. "Mary is mischievous, but she is definitely not an evil presence."

THE TEMPLE THEATER

By the early 1920s, the Hamasa Shrine organization in Meridian had outgrown its meeting place. The leaders of the Hamasa Shrine hired architect Emile Weil to design a new building. Construction of the Grand Ballroom began in 1923. In 1924, the Shriners moved in, even though the remainder of the building was still being built.

The theater was completed later that year. At the time, the theater had the second-largest stage in the United States. The acoustics in the theater were enhanced by the addition of a resonance chamber, which was built as a floor to the orchestra pit. For the next three years, the theater featured only traveling shows. Then, in 1927, the Saenger Corporation in New Orleans leased the building and converted the theater into a silent movie house. Over eighteen hundred seats were installed to accommodate the large crowds of movie fans the Saenger brothers hoped would visit the new theater. Almost immediately, the theater became one of the primary entertainment venues in the region.

In 1928, a Robert Morgan pipe organ was installed to provide musical accompaniment to the silent films. Today, the Robert Morgan pipe organ is one of only two of the same type still installed in their original locations in Mississippi. After the Saenger theater chain's lease expired in 1973, the Hamasa Shrine embarked on an extensive restoration project, which involved cleaning and painting the walls, replacing the carpets and reupholstering the seats. For the next three decades, the Temple Theater saw only limited use. In February 2009, the Shriners sold the Temple Theater and Ballroom to a

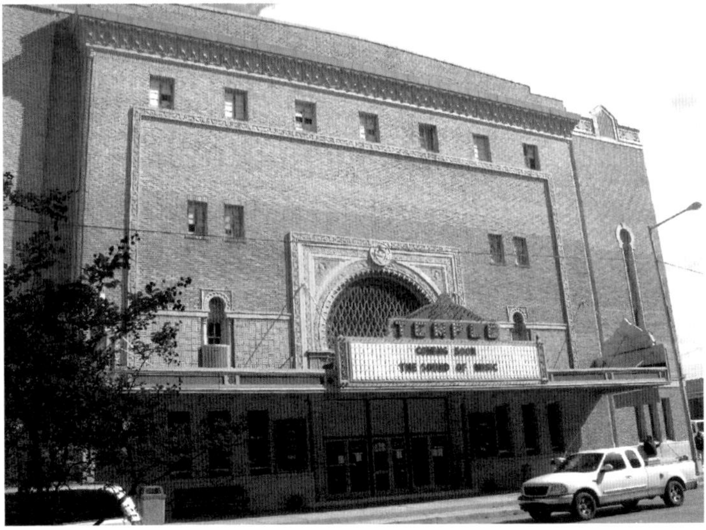

The Temple Theater.

semiretired Texas businessman named Roger Smith, who made additional improvements to the old building. The long list of entertainers who have performed at the Temple Theater since the silent film era includes Tony Bennett, Randy Travis, Elvis Presley, the Oak Ridge Boys, Bill Monroe, Willie Nelson, Alabama, Roy Clark and George Strait. Beginning in the late 2000s, ghosts have offered additional thrills to the Temple Theater's patrons.

Roger Smith says that he heard stories from the employees about the ghostly activity in the building soon after he bought it. One of these workers was the maintenance man, who claimed to have encountered something weird in the attic. A few months after Smith took over the theater, an employee named Lynee Romero had a very unnerving experience in the theater. She said she was walking down the main aisle late one night when she had the eerie feeling that she was being watched. Knowing that she was the only person in the huge building intensified the chills that began creeping up her spine. As she peered into the darkness, Romero glanced up at the upper balcony above the east doorway. Standing in the doorway was a man wearing a top hat. For a very long minute, Romero stood transfixed in the main aisle, staring into the spectral figure's unblinking gaze. Then, slowly, the apparition faded away.

Another employee, Don Allen, had a strange encounter in 2010. He was repairing a light socket when he heard something making scratching noises behind him on the floor. He turned around and saw what he described as the black, shadowy outline of a human being. The ghost dematerialized just a few seconds later.

Entire groups of people have seen the entity as well. One group of seven visitors was in the stage area when they all saw the image of a white-haired man standing in a corner of a room under the stage. A few months later, a group of stagehands working late into the night decided to sleep on the stage instead of going home because they had another performance to prepare for early the next morning. The men were unable to fall asleep because of all the spectral noises that echoed throughout the building. After tossing and turning for about thirty minutes, the stagehands decided to leave. Several have had sightings in and around the stage area since this incident.

The carpenter's shop underneath the stage is haunted as well. This is the area where the scenery for plays and musicals was built. In 2009, a group representing a touring company visited the temple to see if the stage was big enough to accommodate their troupe. Roger Smith was up in his office while the group walked through the theater. About an hour later, the men walked into his office and told him that they had started walking under the stage when they saw a strange-looking man standing in the middle of the room. At the time, there was no one else in the theater. The men refused to go back to the carpenter's shop to look for the man.

A series of tunnels known as the "catacombs" runs under the wooden floors of the Temple Theater. For years, the old tunnels were crammed full of junk. After the tunnels were cleaned out, employees of the theater reported hearing strange noises coming from this underground network of passages.

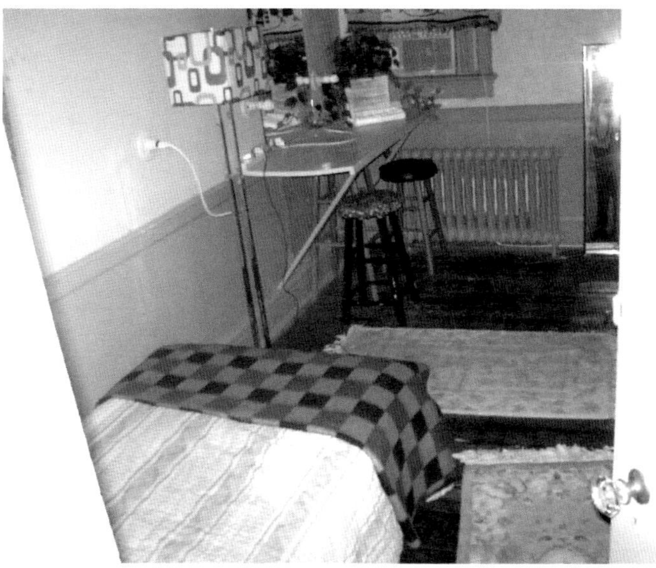

Dressing room in the Temple Theater.

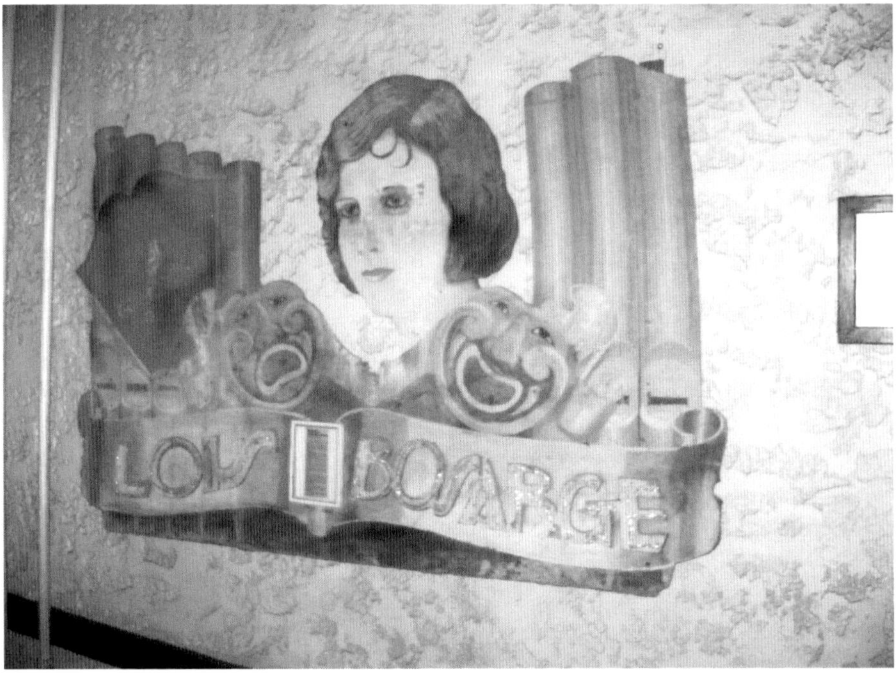

A poster depicting Lois Bosarge, longtime organist at the Temple Theater.

Actors putting on makeup in the dressing rooms have felt very uneasy at times. They say they have heard weird noises in these little rooms when they are all alone. They also have had the eerie feeling that there is someone—or something—in the dressing rooms with them.

No one knows for sure who is haunting the Temple Theater. Some people have identified the ghost as the spirit of an opera singer who was performing on stage one night when he dropped dead of a heart attack. Other people claim to have seen the ghost of a former organist, Miss Lois Bosarge, in the building.

Roger Smith, who lives in the theater, remains skeptical, primarily because he has not had any unusual experiences in the old building. However, the large number of reports that he has received in the two years since becoming director of the Temple Theater have brought him a little closer to becoming a believer. During the last two weeks of October 2010, the Temple capitalized on the public's fascination with the paranormal by offering guided ghost tours of the old building. Ghosts might take their toll on the nerves of the people who have to work around them, but they can be entertaining as well.

MERREHOPE

Merrehope is one of only a handful of antebellum mansions that survived General William Tecumseh Sherman's Valentine's Day arrival in Meridian in 1864. During the Civil War, the twenty-six-room mansion was nothing more than a modest cottage built in 1858 by one of the city's founders, Richard McLemore, for his daughter, Juriah Jackson, and her husband, W.H. Jackson. In 1863, General Joseph H. Johnson acquired the home and made a number of changes to the original structure.

During the Civil War, the cottage became the headquarters for Confederate general Leonidas Polk. A number of General Sherman's officers stayed in the cottage when the Union army attacked Meridian on Valentine's Day 1864.

The house was purchased in 1868 by John Gary, who built the main block. In 1881, the house was sold to J.C. Lloyd. In 1904, the next owner, S.H. Floyd, completely remodeled the house in the Academic Revival style. Floyd added a second story containing a hallway, a bathroom and two servants' rooms. He also added a bathroom, dining room and guest room to the rear of the main block of the house. A giant portico and two-story Ionic columns were built onto the east and south sides of the building. In the 1930s, the old house was divided into eight apartments and converted into a boardinghouse. It continued to serve as a boardinghouse until the 1960s.

In 1968, nine ladies' clubs consolidated to form the Meridian Restorations Foundation, Inc., which purchased the old home. They named the home Merrehope, which is a combination of three words: "Meridian,"

"Restoration" and "Hope." Merrehope was listed on the National Register of Historic Places in 1971. In 1995, the antebellum mansion was designated a Mississippi Landmark. Today, the ladies who run Merrehope raise the funds needed to preserve the old home by giving daily tours and by operating it as a venue for weddings and other special events. Merrehope is a fascinating old home, not just because of its historical significance but also because of the ghosts that are reputed to reside there.

The first hint of haunted activity at Merrehope occurred right after the old mansion was first opened to the general public in 1973. Fonda Rush had just started working as a hostess at Merrehope during her last year in college when she decided to show the house to her boyfriend. One afternoon, they pulled up into the side parking lot. They could tell by the absence of cars that no one else was there. The couple got out of the car and walked over to the front porch. Fonda walked up the side steps, and her boyfriend walked up the front steps. When they walked onto the front porch and looked inside the front window, both of them saw a young woman dressed in an 1870s-period

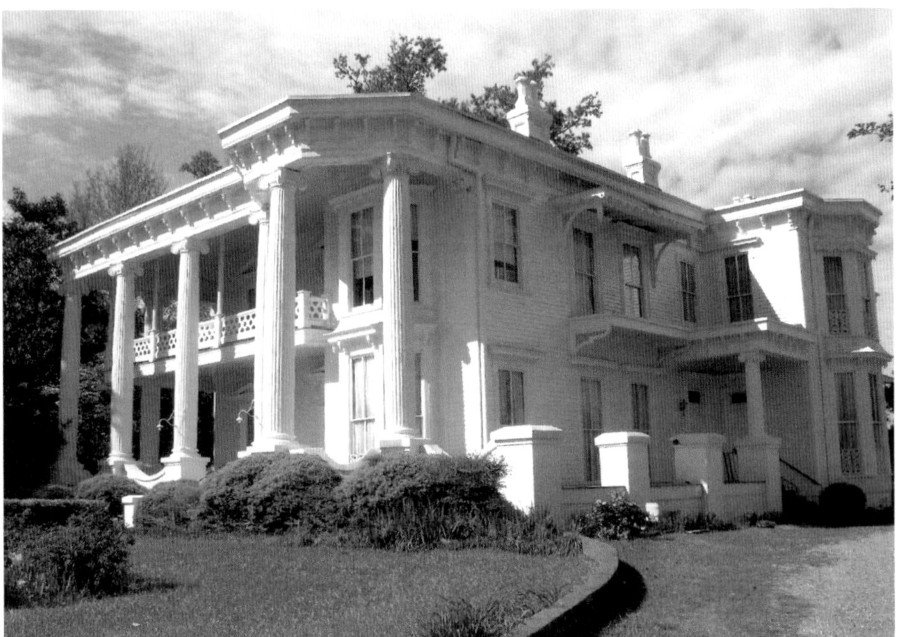

Merrehope, Meridian's only existing antebellum mansion.

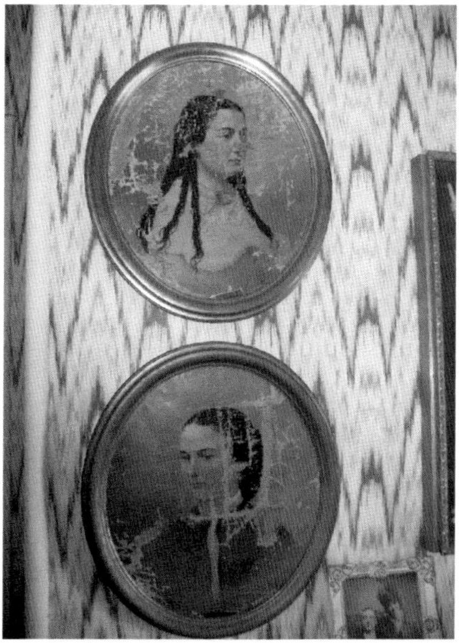

Portraits of Eugenia and Pristina Gary in the Museum Room.

hoop skirt standing in the front parlor. Sensing that something was not quite right, they both ran back into the car and drove off.

A few days later, one of the board members showed Fonda a couple of paintings that the foundation had acquired from the Gary family. They were paintings of two of John Gary's daughters—Eugenia and Pristina—who had died of tuberculosis in Livingston. When Fonda looked at Eugenia's portrait, she realized—to her horror—that she was staring into the face of the young girl she and her boyfriend had seen at Merrehope.

Years later, Fonda's daughter also had an encounter with the ghost of Eugenia at Merrehope. One October, Fonda and her daughter were serving as hostesses for a Halloween party. Both of them were wearing period dresses. During a lull in the party, Fonda's daughter walked out onto the balcony outside of the Museum Room. Suddenly, she had the uneasy feeling that she was being watched. She turned around and saw a young woman wearing a late nineteenth-century dress standing in the room, staring out the window. When the girl remembered that this was the room where Eugenia Gary's portrait was hanging, shivers began crawling up and down her spine.

The ghost of Eugenia has proven to be the most active spirit in Merrehope. One day, a lady who was on a tour with her friend asked Fonda, "You have a ghost here, don't you?" Fonda asked the lady what gave her that idea, and she replied, "Because my friend and I heard her singing in the bathroom connected to the Bride's Room." One afternoon, a woman was walking around the back of Merrehope in search of her husband, a carpenter who had been working on the house for several days. When she finally caught up with him, she told him that she had seen a woman in an old-fashioned dress staring out of one of the upper windows. He replied that he had been alone all afternoon. One hot summer day, when the air conditioner was shut off for repairs, a couple of tourists standing in front of Eugenia's portrait complained of feeling cold. Back in the late 1990s, a docent opened up

Merrehope one morning and was surprised to find a windowpane in one of the second-floor rooms broken. She looked out the window and noticed a long ladder and an open box of tools scattered all over the lawn. The docent concluded that Eugenia must have scared away a burglar while he was trying to break into the house. Eugenia has also been blamed for playing the piano and setting off the motion detectors.

Meridian author and longtime Merrehope board member Anne McKee recalled a bizarre incident that occurred in December 1998. Eight honors students from West Lauderdale High School had been invited to Merrehope to assist with the trimming of the trees. Anne assigned one young man the task of decorating one of the trees upstairs. About an hour later, the boy walked down the stairs and informed Anne that he was not going back upstairs anymore because he had seen a young woman with dark hair standing in the Museum Room. He said she was wearing a white dress. A hostess named Wanda Clay asked the young man to take her upstairs so that she could see for herself where the ghost had appeared to him. He led her down the hall to the doorway of the Museum Room. Pointing into one of the corners of the

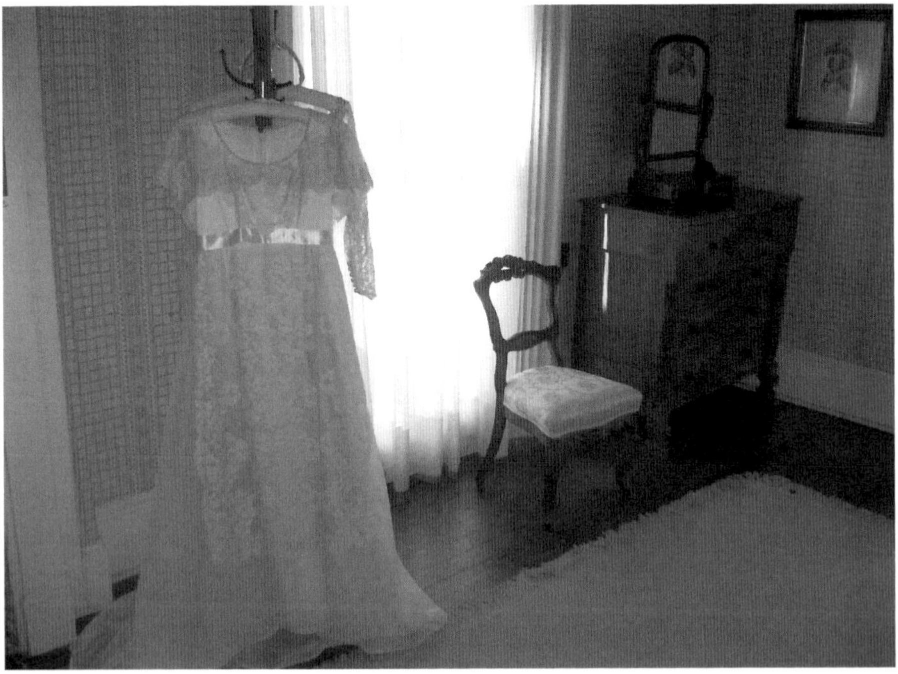

Visitors have heard ghostly singing coming from the bathroom attached to the Bride's Room.

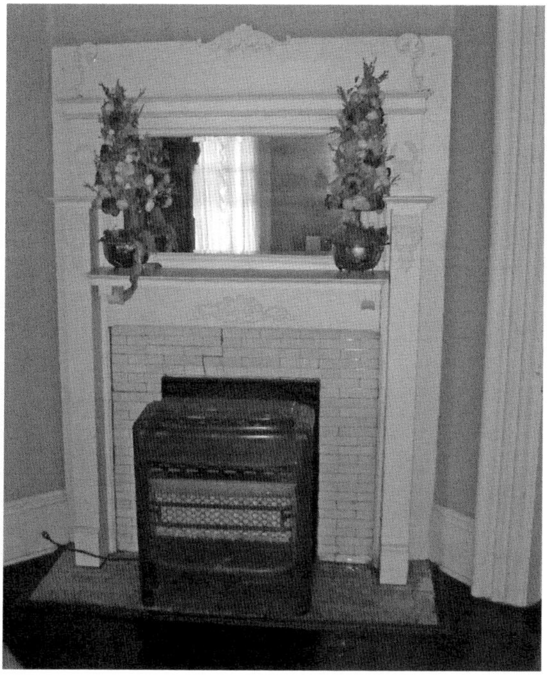

A retired teacher boarding in the Periwinkle Room shot a row of empty whiskey bottles placed on the mantel of this fireplace. He then turned the gun on himself.

room, he said, "There she is." Wanda asked, "Where?" and the boy pointed again in the same direction. Even though she did not see anything, Wanda was convinced that the boy had seen something.

A group of teachers from Butler, Alabama, decided to take a tour of Merrehope after a busy day of Christmas shopping. The ladies were standing in the Museum Room, listening to one of the docents, when a closet door opened on its own. Unperturbed by the door's strange behavior, the docent walked over to the closet and shut the door. She tried to open the door again but was unable to because the wood seemed to have swollen. The docent, who had never had any trouble with the closet door, advised the ladies to leave because Eugenia apparently did not want them in the Museum Room. While the ladies were examining the antiques in the adjoining room, the doorbell rang. The docent stopped talking long enough to go downstairs to answer the door. When she returned, the teachers could tell by the puzzled look on her face that something out of the ordinary had just occurred. The docent said that when she opened the door, no one was there. She took this incident as a sign that Eugenia did not want her or the teachers upstairs. The group walked down the stairs to the first floor and did not have any more weird encounters for the remainder of their tour.

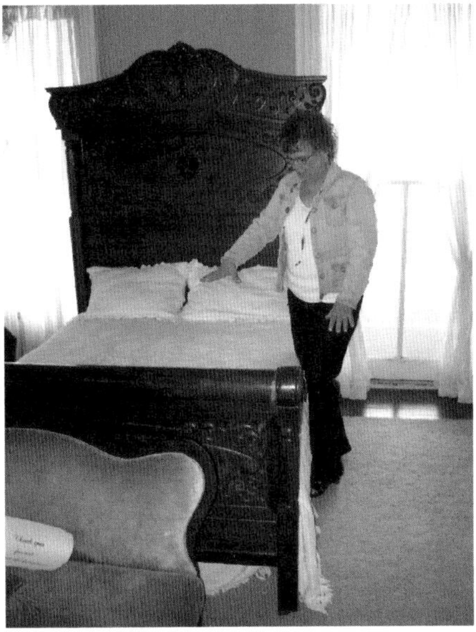

Docent Peggy Shoffiette points at the bed in the Periwinkle Room where the impression of a human form occasionally appears.

Longtime docent Donna White was never uncomfortable working in Merrehope, with the exception of the Periwinkle Room, where a retired schoolteacher shot himself back in the 1940s, when Merrehope was being used as a boardinghouse. Shortly after she started working at the old mansion, she discovered something unusual about the antique bed. "After I opened up at 9:00 a.m.," she said, "I went into the Periwinkle Room, and I discovered the impression where someone had slept in the bed. I had straightened out the bed before I left the day before, so I knew that something weird had happened." The suicidal spirit has also been blamed for assaulting a guest at Merrehope. A group of visitors was on the first floor, listening to a docent talk about the history of the mansion, when a young man standing by the foot of the stairs sucked in his breath very quickly. When the docent walked over to him and asked him what was wrong, he replied that it felt like someone had punched him very hard in the stomach.

The first scientific investigation of Merrehope was conducted on October 30, 2002. The all-night stay at Merrehope was sponsored by local radio station WOKK, which invited four teachers from Patrician Academy to tag along—Linda Couch, Sheela McBride, Lolane Lewis and Pam Hearst. The investigation was led by Donovan Murphy, a paranormal investigator from Birmingham, Alabama. In his first walk-through of the old mansion, he was unable to collect any EVPs or any significant fluctuations in the electromagnetic field with his EMF detector. However, between 2:00 and 4:30 a.m., while everyone else was asleep, Murphy heard "bumping and thumping" noises in the rooms upstairs. "I checked on everybody who was asleep, and nobody appeared to have gone to the bathroom," Murphy said.

The strongest paranormal activity that evening was centered on a curio cabinet in the Museum Room. At midnight, I was sitting in the parlor on the first floor with the four guests from Patrician Academy and two disc jockeys from WOKK, Scotty Ray Boyd and Debbie Alexander. We were watching the computer monitor, which was being fed images from a camera that had been set up in the Museum Room upstairs. Nothing unusual appeared on the computer screen until 12:35 a.m., when all five of us saw the door to the curio cabinet in the Museum Room open all by itself. Thinking that someone was playing a prank, I ran upstairs and looked in all of the rooms on the second floor. No one was there but me.

Donovan Murphy had his own bizarre experience with the curio cabinet. When he walked into the Museum Room to reset his camera at 4:00 a.m., the door to the curio cabinet opened on its own. Murphy was so unnerved that he ran all the way downstairs. Scotty Ray Boyd's assessment of the curio cabinet's strange behavior summed up the way we all felt:

> *If you heard somebody say that the door opened by itself, you'd think they were crazy. But I saw it happen on the video camera when nothing else was in the room. You might be able to explain the door opening by itself due to the house shifting or maybe an unlevel floor, but it wouldn't close up and latch up by itself.*

On October 27, 2004, I made my second overnight visit to Merrehope with WOKK radio anchors Debbie Alexander and Scotty Ray Boyd and several guests. Although we were supposed to stay at the neighboring F.W. Williams House, we found ourselves spending most of our time at Merrehope for two reasons. First of all, the F.W. Williams House has no operating bathrooms and Merrehope does. Second, the F.W. Williams House does not have Merrehope's haunted reputation. After we walked next door to Merrehope, a few sweeps with my EMF detector convinced me that Merrehope was the place we should be investigating, not the F.W. Williams House.

At 10:00 p.m., Debbie Alexander and I were upstairs in the Bride's Room. As I walked around the room, I was not getting very significant readings. However, when I placed the EMF detector on the antique bed, the meter jumped to 17.8 and then climbed to 18.5 within a few seconds. I moved the EMF detector to different parts of the bed and found that the readings were stronger in some places than in others. At one point, the meter climbed all the way to 30.0. Debbie and I returned to the Bride's Room an hour later and found that the readings had dropped way down to 1.4. Then, at about midnight, we returned once again, and the meter spiked to 25.0 at the foot of the bed. The fluctuations in the readings have convinced me that they were not caused by some unknown power source.

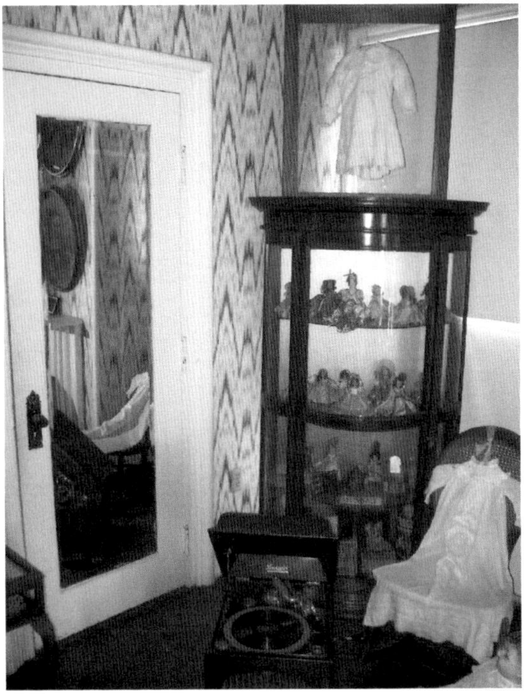

Left: The door to this curio cabinet swung open during a paranormal investigation of Merrehope.

Below: The parlor where overnight visitors at Merrehope encountered the ghost of a very friendly cat.

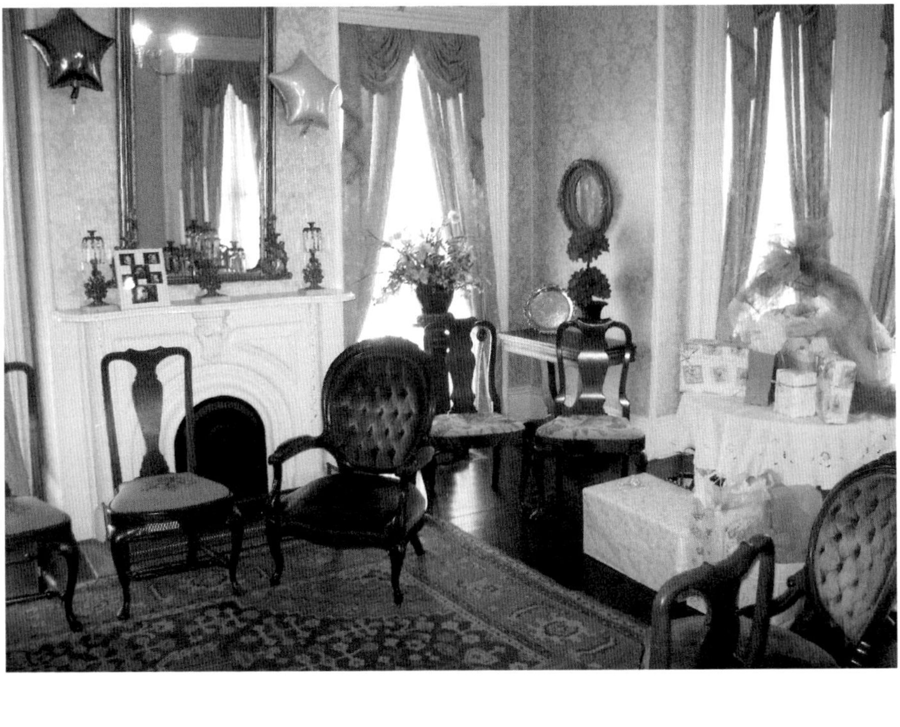

Our second weird experience in Merrehope that night occurred in the same parlor where Donna had smelled the perfume and felt the drop in temperature a year before. I was standing in the parlor at 1:00 a.m. talking to Marianne Todd, a local photographer, when she told me that she was experiencing a strange sensation of cold air at her feet. I held the EMF detector at ground level and got a reading of 14.5. The high readings stopped about six inches above Marianne's ankle. She also said she felt a slight pressure on her leg. Another guest stood at the same spot and reported feeling cold in the same place on her leg. I was puzzled by the readings until Marianne suggested that the entity could have been the ghost of Eugenia's cat. Once again, I am certain that the readings were not produced by a power source. Two years before, I had crawled under the house and found no wiring under the parlor.

Nothing else of note happened that night. We left Merrehope the next morning feeling that we had come no closer to solving the mysteries of the old mansion than we had two years before. It is comforting to know, though, that the gentle spirit that looks after her beloved home is still on the job.

A few weeks after our investigation, Marianne Todd showed me several wedding photographs she had taken on the lawn outside of Merrehope a few weeks before our investigation. "When I blew up the photographs, I discovered faces in one of the windows on the side of the house," Mary Ann said. "I could see the face of a boy, a girl, a cat's face and a demonic figure with horns and flared nostrils. I took several pictures in rapid succession, and in each picture, the faces seemed to change position." I must admit that when I examined the photographs, I had difficulty making out all the faces Mary Ann had seen, with the exception of the cat's face, which was clearly outlined in the glass.

On December 7, 2008, dental hygienist Regina Ziller took her three young sons to Merrehope for its Trees of Christmas celebration. "Both of my younger sons were eager to go," Regina said. "One of them had decorated one of the trees with his class at school. My older son didn't seem to care about the trees, so I just told him to walk around and look for the ghosts." At the end of their tour, Regina decided to take a photograph with her cellphone of her older son standing in front of the Christmas tree in the foyer. "I asked one of the ladies to turn on the light in the room," she said. "She tried several times, but it just wouldn't turn on." After a minute or so, Regina's son started to feel cold. "That was really odd," Regina said, "because it had been really hot in the house the entire time we were there."

When Regina and her boys returned home, she decided to look at the picture she had taken on her computer. "I could tell there was a little white glob by my son's head," Regina said.

> *When I zoomed in, I could see a woman's face floating right next to my son's face. You could see her forehead, her eyes and nose and part of her mouth. You could even tell that her hair had been parted down the middle. For the next two weeks, I just stared at the photo on my cellphone and asked myself, "How could this face have appeared on my camera?" Finally, I concluded that it had to be a ghost.*

The entire time Regina and her boys were walking through the old antebellum mansion, they were joking about how eager they were to begin taking pictures of ghosts. "I don't think it's a coincidence that one of the spirits showed up on my telephone photo," Regina said.

Regina was so proud of her weird photograph that she showed it to her co-workers in the dentist's office. "Unfortunately, I accidentally washed the phone in the washing machine, so the only copy I have of the photo is on my son's camera. He tried to copy the photo as it appeared on the computer screen, so it's not very good. My son told me that I was more upset about losing the original photograph than I was about the camera itself." For the past two years, Regina asked her sons if they would like to return to Merrehope. Two of them said yes; one of them said no.

Merrehope is a survivor. It has held its head up high through the Civil War, through a devastating tornado and hurricane and through years of neglect. The still-beautiful antebellum home stands today as a testament to the resilient spirit of the people of Meridian. Indeed, at least two of its former occupants seem to be reluctant to "give up the ghost," so to speak.

THE RILEY CENTER (THE GRAND OPERA HOUSE)

Meridian's Grand Opera House had its inception in the minds of two Jewish immigrants from Germany. In the 1880s, two half brothers—Marks and Lee Rothenberg—opened a department store on Front Street, not far from the railroad tracks. They were convinced that the idea of having an opera house would appeal to the other European immigrants living in Meridian, most of whom shared the brothers' love of opera and other types of musical entertainment. They also believed that the same railroads that had transformed Meridian into a major transportation center could bring opera companies, performers and opera lovers to the city.

The structure they had in mind would conform to the standard required for the designation of "Grand Opera House." The stage was thirty feet wide and fifty feet deep. A department store occupied the first floor of the building; the opera house was on the second floor. The Rothenbergs intended to use profits from the retail store to help support the opera house. Employees of the opera house would perform double duty, selling tickets and building scenery on the second floor and selling retail goods on the first floor.

The beautiful late Victorian Empire/Romanesque–style building opened on December 17, 1890. Theatergoers who attended a German-language performance of Johann Strauss's *The Gypsy Baron* by a company from New York were awestruck by the seats upholstered in wine velvet and white and gold walls accented in gold leaf. The performance was framed by a thirty-five-foot-high proscenium arch with an ornate painted border. For thirty years, the Grand Opera House offered the residents of Meridian a

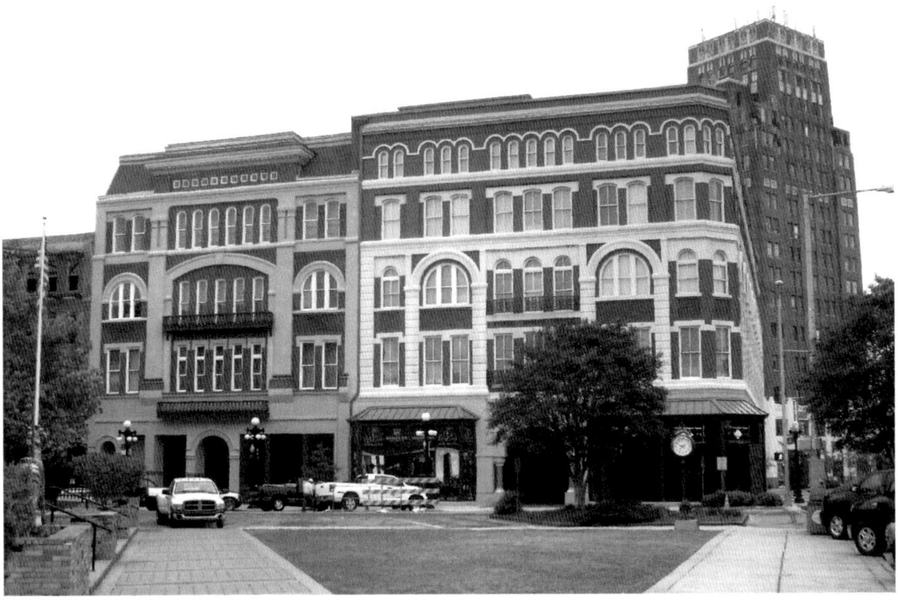

The Riley Center, formerly known as the Grand Opera House.

wide variety of plays, operas, vaudeville acts and concerts. Thanks to the railroad, the people of Meridian were able to see performers who normally performed back east, such as Enrico Caruso, Lon Chaney Sr., John Gilbert, Norma Shearer and Helen Hayes. Minstrel troupes featuring both white performers in blackface and African American companies, such as Black Pattie, performed on the stage of the Grand Opera House.

The advent of motion pictures spelled the end of vaudeville but the beginning of a new phase in the history of the Grand Opera House. In May 1920, the Grand Opera House was transformed into a movie theater. The renovations included dividing the gallery into two areas. The grand opening was held on June 7, 1920. The management called the films "pictodramas" to add a veneer of class to the theater. To make the theater more comfortable for the increasing numbers of moviegoers, the owners installed a cooling system.

Ironically, the 1920s also witnessed the end of the Grand Opera House. It was leased by Saenger Films of New Orleans. The lease was supposed to last thirty years, but four years later, the company decided to convert the opera house into an office building after purchasing the Temple Theater. However, the company's plans fell through because Levi Rothenberg, the former owner of the opera house, had placed a clause in the lease stating that the opera house could only be used as a theater. Saenger Films refused to continue leasing the opera house at $1,000 per month and moved out of the building. After a long court battle, the judge decided in Rothenberg's favor. However, the death of Levi Rothenberg, the bankruptcy of Saenger Films and the Great Depression sealed the fate of the building. The Grand Opera House closed its doors in 1927.

For the next sixty years, the Grand Opera House slipped into obscurity. The staircase connecting the opera house with the outside world was removed. A variety of businesses occupied the first floor of the building. The second floor, where the opera house was located, was sealed up. Metal siding was installed on the outside in an attempt to modernize the building. The revival of the Grand Opera House began in 1988, when it was sold to the Historic Meridian Foundation. In the late 1980s and early 1990s, tours were given inside the opera house in an attempt to raise money for its restoration. On March 11, 1993, the Grand Opera House was designated as the official State Grand Opera House of Mississippi.

The opera house's rebirth seemed uncertain until 1999, when the president of Mississippi State University, Malcom Portera, initiated efforts to restore the Grand Opera House and the Marks-Rothenberg department store on the first floor. In 2000, the Riley Foundation's donation of $10 million helped make the restoration of the Grand Opera House a reality. The Riley Center donated another $2.1 million for technology upgrades. With contributions from the city, county and federal governments, the remodeling of the $25 million MSU Riley Center for Education and Performing Arts was completed in 2006. Today, the Riley Center includes a theater that has seating for 950 people. The fully restored building also has an exhibit hall and boardrooms.

Rumors about the ghost in the Grand Opera House first surfaced during the 1980s. Elliott Street, the former director of the opera house, became one of the first people to encounter the ghost when he brought his girlfriend into the theater after a date. In an interview with *Meridian Star* reporter Jennifer Jacob Brown, Street said that they walked across the stage through the big metal doors. "No lights had been rigged yet, so it was really dark," Street said.

> *I was making my way with a flashlight over to the little pull-chain light bulbs—it was in midsummer—and I walked into a cold spot. I looked down, and the hair on my arm was standing up. Now I don't know if that was my own fear that rushed through me and made my hair stand up, or if it was something else, but I had never seen my hair stand up quite like that.*

The couple stopped walking, and Street's date said, "There is a female spirit here [that] means us no harm, and it doesn't mind us being here." Street suggested that they explore a different part of the opera house instead. He is convinced that the female ghost haunting the theater is the spirit of the woman whose portrait appears above the stage.

A few weeks later, Street's suspicions that the opera house was haunted were confirmed by a woman who asked him for a tour. During the tour, she told Street that years before, when she worked downtown, she would sneak into the "sealed" opera house and eat her lunch on the wooden staircase. Several times, she heard a woman singing, even though she was certain that she was the only one inside the opera house at the time.

Fonda Rush's children, Sara and Elliott, were inside the opera house one evening while their mother was giving a tour when they heard a woman singing. The singing seemed to be coming from the stage. However, neither Sara nor Elliott could see anyone on the stage, and they could not understand the words of the song she was singing. After the singing stopped, the children heard footsteps, as if someone were leaving the stage.

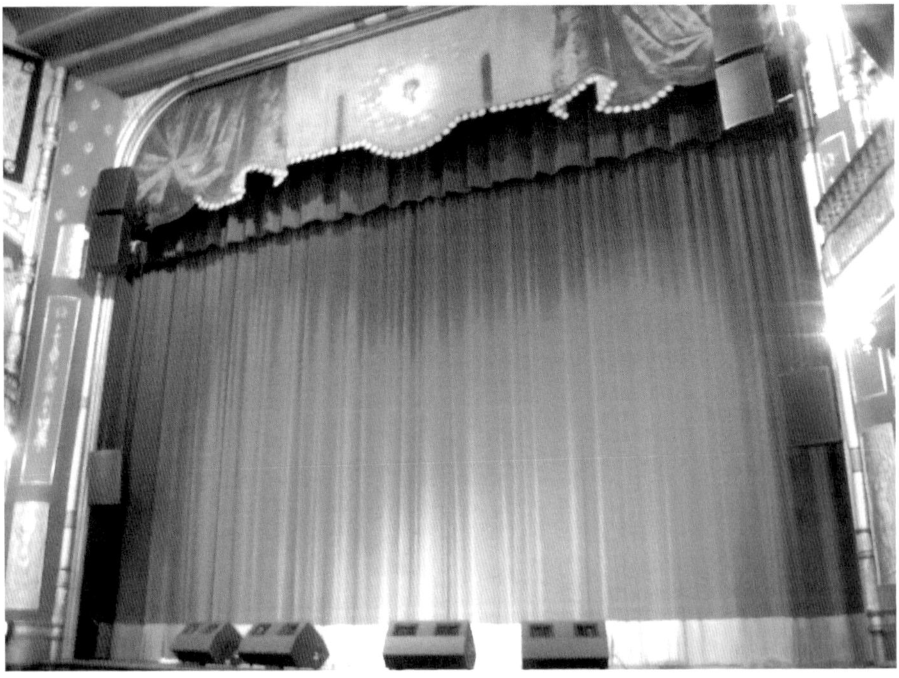

A portrait of the "singing ghost" hangs above the stage in the Riley Center.

Fonda had her own uncanny experiences after she started giving tours of the Grand Opera House. One day she ran into a cold spot. At the time, she recalled the stories others had told her of encountering cold spots in the backstage area. She had another bizarre experience a few months later while she was guiding a group of ladies through the opera house. The group was standing in the auditorium, listening to Fonda, when suddenly her presentation was interrupted by the sound of shattering glass. She immediately thought that a huge pane of glass had fallen out of one of the windows in the front of the building. She combed the entire opera house but was unable to find any pieces of broken glass.

After the Grand Opera House opened as the Riley Center, other people began having ghostly experiences. Most of the eyewitnesses were staff members, some of whom saw a lady in a white gown, heard footsteps on the stage and felt cold drafts. In July 2010, a female security guard was inside the ladies' room on the first floor when she distinctly heard the lilting voice of a woman singing. Most of the paranormal activity seems to take place on the second floor.

Penny Kemp, former marketing director for the MSU Riley Center for Education and the Performing Arts, said that in the beginning she enjoyed hearing the ghost stories connected with the opera house but did not really believe in the ghost. However, she changed her mind about the ghost one evening when she was standing at the second-floor entrance to the auditorium, giving instructions to a group of volunteers who had just started working there. She had just talked about the importance of keeping the audience safe during performances when she felt a tap on her shoulder. She immediately turned around and said, "Excuse me," but no one was there. "I wasn't scared," Penny said. "It was more of a reassuring kind of tap on the shoulder."

In 2007, a group of ghost hunters from New Orleans conducted a formal investigation of the Riley Center. Their leader was a woman who called herself "Bloody Mary." Dennis Sankovich, director of the Riley Center, assisted the group as they did their walk-through in the old opera house. Like most members of the group, Sankovich captured a number of orbs with his digital camera. When Sankovich enlarged one of his photographs, the face of a woman was clearly visible inside one of the orbs.

The *Meridian Star* ran the story of a bizarre encounter inside the Riley Center in its September 15, 2009 edition. According to reporter Jennifer Jacobs Brown, two members of the cleaning staff, Patricia Smith and her daughter, Jamecia, saw the ghost of a woman on the second floor, where

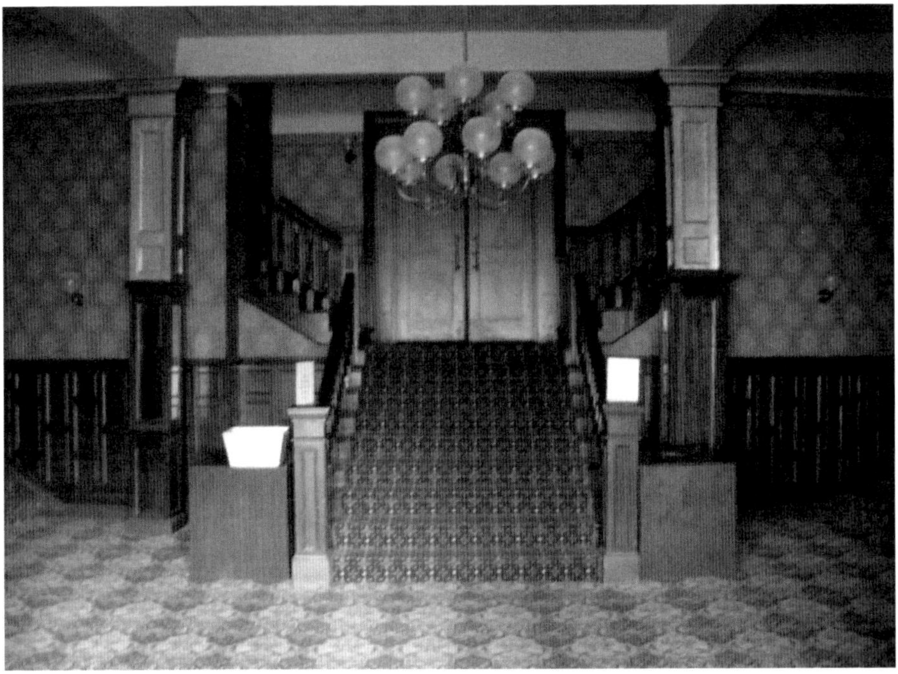

Penny Kemp felt a reassuring hand on her shoulder while standing outside the entrance to the auditorium.

most of the sightings took place. Charlotte Taberaux, director of education, described the women's unsettling experience:

> *They said she wore a white, flowing dress and had long, dark hair put up in an old-fashioned style, kind of like the lady* [whose portrait hangs above] *the curtain. What's funny is, that's the exact description another worker gave years ago, and nobody who saw her on Monday knows that he described her like that.*

Although a large number of people have made the acquaintance of the ghostly presence inside the Riley Center, none believed that the spirit was malevolent. Both Street and Sankovich experienced feelings of benevolence when they sensed they had met something from the "other side." Even though neither man is 100 percent convinced that the Riley Center is really haunted, they are both grateful for the publicity that the ghost stories have brought to the old opera house.

MERIDIAN CITY HALL

Located at 601 Twenty-fourth Avenue, Meridian City Hall was designed by architect P.J. Krouse, who began work on the project on April 15, 1914. The new building was to replace the previous city hall, which was built in 1885. Work on the Beaux Arts building was completed in 1915. The city jail occupied the first floor, the mayor's office was on the second floor and the Civic Auditorium took up most of the third floor. Some Meridian residents still remember listening to piano recitals in the Civic Auditorium. The city jail remained on the first floor from 1915 until the current jail was built in 1977.

The appearance of the building changed very little until the 1950s, when a number of "modern" touches were added. When air conditioning was added, drop ceilings had to be installed to create room for the ducts. As a result, the original plaster moulding was hidden for years. Workmen filled the windows on the first floor with concrete. Large chambers were divided up into smaller offices by means of wood paneling. Some of the building's most beautiful features were painted over, such as the terra cotta tiles and Scagliola columns. Workers covered up marble and wooden floors with linoleum and replaced the grand staircase with an elevator.

When consultants were hired to investigate the faulty HVAC systems in city hall in 2003, they discovered so many other problems that the city decided to initiate an extensive renovation of the entire building. The contractor's overall plan was to restore city hall to its 1915 appearance. Most of the remodeling involved removing the modern "improvements" that had

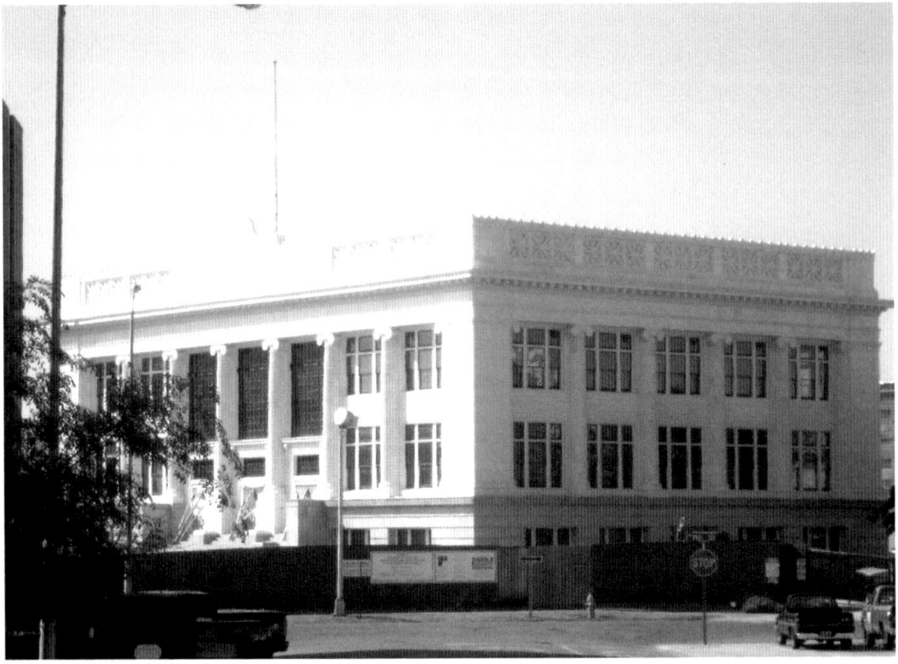

Meridian City Hall undergoing restoration in 2011.

been made approximately fifty years before. The plan involved returning the cross and jack sunscreens to their original black color; replacing all vinyl and plastic in the interior with plaster, wood, glass and marble; replacing the aluminum windows with mahogany replicas of the originals; and moving the elevator to make room for the restored grand marble staircase. By 2010, the projected cost of the renovations—$7–8 million—had more than doubled to $17 million, at least partially because the Mississippi Department of Archives and History required that any features of the building that were salvageable had to be repaired instead of replaced. As of 2011, the remodeling of Meridian City Hall was not yet completed.

Former historical preservationist Fonda Rush, whose office was located in Meridian City Hall in the 1990s, described the building as a

> *very strange place, especially the first floor, which was being used as a storage area and as a custodial area when I was there. The jail cells were still there. Those of us who wrote grants often stayed late because we couldn't get much done during the day. We were always being interrupted.*

Sometimes at night, we'd hear voices on the first floor and movement in the building. We knew we weren't alone. We would pick up the phone and call the police. We always told the police we were hearing these strange noises when we were in the building by ourselves.

Fonda recalled one particular night when she was staying late inside city hall working on a grant by herself:

I was starting down the stairwell—those of us who worked on the third floor used the stairs more than we did the elevator—and just as I stepped onto the landing on the second floor, one of the windows where people paid their bills at night started shaking. First one shook, and then when I started walking past the second window, it shook too. It was as if someone was touching them and making them rattle as I walked by, so I hurried down the stairs. As I unlocked the door and locked it back again, I heard voices. After that incident, I didn't really stay very late. Later on, the custodians told me that they too heard voices on the first floor when they came into work.

Fonda's most bizarre experience occurred late one afternoon when she was in Mayor Jimmy Kemp's office, talking to him about a project he was working on. "There was a spotlight as you were coming through the door to his office," Fonda said.

Jimmy Kemp was sitting on that side of the desk, and I was sitting on the other side. We were talking about Mayor John Parker. He was mayor of Meridian twice. One of his big projects was getting the new city hall built. He was elected mayor again in the mid-1920s. Mayor Parker was on a trip to Hattiesburg on a train and had a heart attack. He was laid in state in city hall. He was a very well-loved mayor. Well, every time we would talk about John Parker, Jimmy Kemp would stop talking and say, "Did you notice that?" I'd say, "See what?" He'd say, "That light behind you came on when we were talking about Mayor Parker, and it would go off when we would stop." We had a good laugh about it.

Fonda thinks she accidentally uncovered the identity of the ghost one day when she was helping close out the old vault downstairs. "This was just before I left and began working for Habitat for Humanity in 1999," Fonda said.

> *We went through stuff that was considered historical, and we found two reports of deaths in the jail. In these records, I read that a man and a woman had died in the jail. The report was vague about how the woman had died, but it said that he was drunk and was smoking a cigarette in bed. He fell asleep, and his mattress caught on fire. The man burned to death. These deaths occurred during or shortly after World War I. While I was reading, I recalled hearing some people say that they had heard the voices of a man and a woman talking at night in city hall.*

Although Fonda confesses to having been "spooked out" on more than one occasion, she never really felt as if her life was in danger while she worked at city hall. She felt especially close to the spirit of Mayor John Parker. "I think Parker felt like city hall was his because he oversaw its construction," Fonda said. "Also, he was laid in state in city hall, so maybe he feels like it's his home."

The Threefoot Building

For years, people have joked that the tallest building in Meridian, Mississippi, is the Threefoot Building. This sixteen-story, Art Deco–style structure was built in 1929 by a family of German-Jewish immigrants who "Americanized" their name—Dreyfus—by changing it to the word's English translation: "Threefoot." The building was erected at a cost of $750,000 on the site of the Threefoot Bros. and Co. hardware store. Construction was completed just before the stock market crash on Black Tuesday—October 29, 1929.

Sporting a polychrome terra cotta and granite exterior, the Threefoot Building was one of the most impressive structures in the entire city. The Threefoot family's fortune declined during the Great Depression, and they were forced to sell the building. A number of different people owned the Threefoot Building over the next several decades. However, the challenge of renting out all of the building's 250 offices proved to be extremely difficult. The construction of the Village Fair Mall just a few blocks away spelled doom for the old building. By the 1990s, the Threefoot Building had been abandoned, for the most part.

The Threefoot Building enjoyed a revival of sorts in 2002, when Meridian initiated its annual showcase of works by local artists. Named after the city's most recognizable landmark, the Threefoot Festival was combined with the Arts in the Park Festival in 2009.

In 2006, the City of Meridian bought the historic building from developer Howard Robbins for $1.2 million in the hope that another developer would

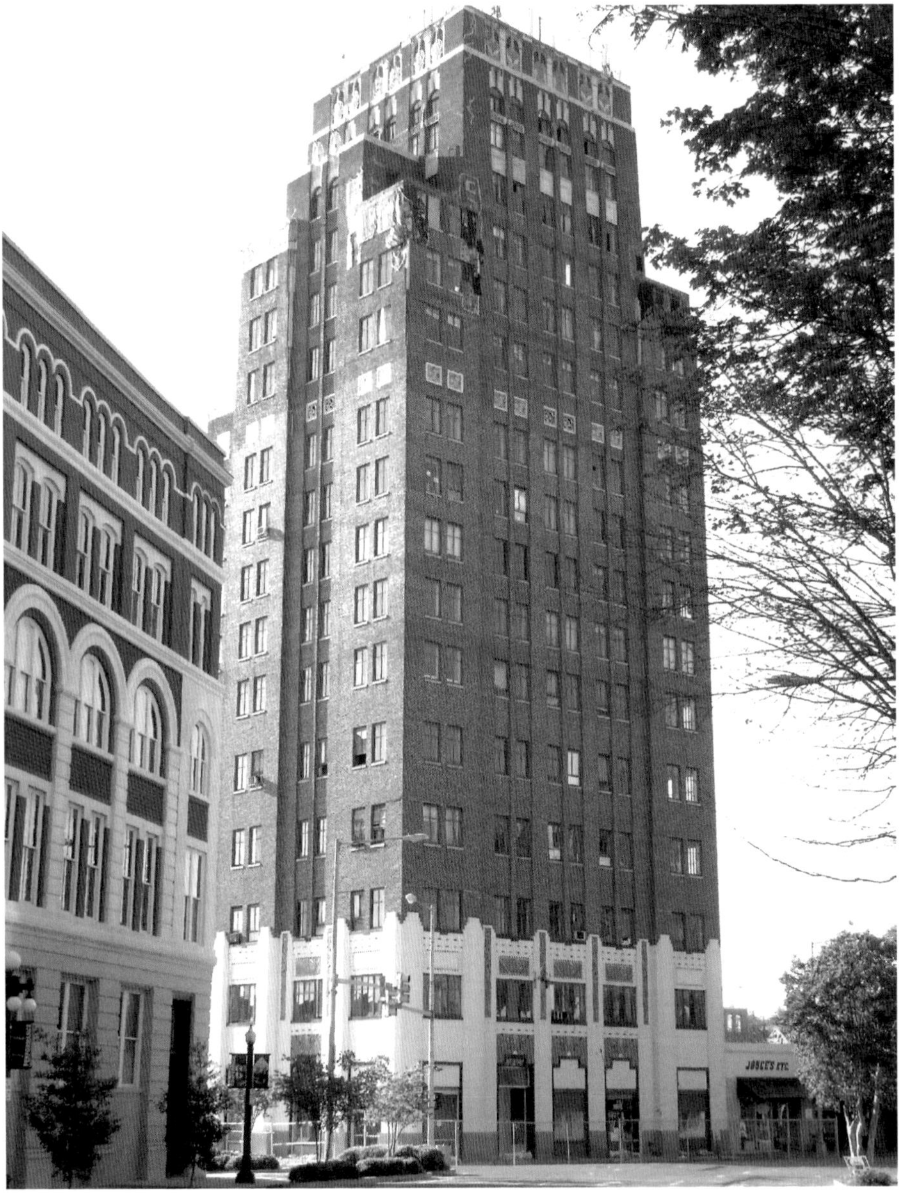

The Threefoot Building.

be interested in restoring it. In 2009, Historic Restoration Inc. from New Orleans undertook the project. The architectural firm signed an agreement with Mayor John Robert Smith and the city in January 2009. The terms of the agreement stipulated that the city would pay for $14 million of the $55 million cost of restoring the building. However, when the new mayor, Cheri Barry, took office in July 2009, she said that because of the nation's dire economic downturn, Meridian would not be able to provide its share of the funding. Consequently, HRI's agreement with Meridian was terminated later that year.

Plans to demolish the historic landmark were slowed down when the Mississippi Heritage Trust placed it on its list of "11 Most Endangered Historic Places in Mississippi" in June 2010. At the time, the Threefoot Building was also on the National Register of Historic Places. In October 2010, the Mississippi Department of Archives and History awarded Meridian a $150,000 grant to study the feasibility of rehabilitating the building. In addition, Watkins Development was hired to investigate the possibility of reviving the Threefoot Building and the remainder of downtown Meridian as well.

The people who want to save the Threefoot Building argue that it is the city's most visible symbol. Indeed, generations of Meridian residents have worked and done business in the offices located inside the building. Many people still recall how nervous they felt waiting to see the dentist in his office in the Threefoot Building. For decades, it was an integral part of the daily lives of thousands of people. The memories embedded within the walls speak to the need to give the once-proud edifice the respect it deserves. The ghosts that are reputed to walk the dusty, debris-strewn halls of the building would make the same argument.

Rumors of ghosts inside the locked doors of the Threefoot Building have been circulating around Meridian for years. Workmen who were granted access to the building after it was closed whispered tales about strange things that happened to them while they were there. Fonda Rush, former historical preservationist of Meridian, made the acquaintance of someone who had personal encounters with the ghosts in the Threefoot Building. She said that when she worked for the city in the 1990s, she received a phone call from one of the owners of the Threefoot Building, a man from Mobile. At the time, the property was being managed by a lady he had hired to live there and take care of it. She and her husband lived in an apartment at the top of the Threefoot Building. The owner of the building asked Fonda to speak to the woman, who was convinced that the Threefoot Building was haunted.

"She asked me to come over," Fonda said.

> *She and her husband had a lot of things going on, and they believed the building was haunted. They had no real sightings, just uneasy feelings. Doors would close and open. They would place an object in a room, and it would get moved to a different location the next day. She said they would hear noises during the night—bumps, footsteps, voices. The building was already vacant by that time, so this was pretty weird.*

The manager asked Fonda if she knew about any deaths that had occurred in the building. At the time, Fonda did not know of anyone who had died there, but her curiosity was aroused. "I began to ask around," Fonda said, "and found out there was a lady who jumped off the Threefoot Building and committed suicide. My mother is the one who told me. I think it happened in the 1950s. She was the aunt of a guy who worked on the city's street cleaning crew."

In 2011, the Threefoot Building stands vacant, a dilapidated vestige of its former glory. In 2008, Mayor John Robert Smith released a report stating that the instability of the façade posed a safety hazard for people walking or driving past the building. In an article that appeared in the August 30, 2009 edition of the *Meridian Star*, reporter Jennifer Jacobs Brown wrote that the interior of the building was in even worse shape. In some places, the floors were covered with filthy patches of carpeting. In other parts of the building, nothing covered the floors except dirt and debris. The walls were coated with peeling coats of old paint and cheap sheets of sheetrock. Scarred, broken pieces of furniture could be found everywhere. The elevators still worked, but they were so rickety-looking that only the most courageous or foolish passengers would attempt to ride in them. An underground stream flowing through the basement boiler room still flooded occasionally. Brown made it clear that renovating the Threefoot Building would be a massive effort requiring thousands of dollars and man-hours.

However, hope for the old Meridian landmark might be on the horizon. In a front-page article that appeared in the June 12, 2011 edition of the *Meridian Star*, Jennifer Jacob Brown reported that Jason Goree, vice-president of Watkins Development, expressed interest in renovating the Threefoot Building into a part-residential, part-commercial development. The Threefoot Building would become a catalyst for downtown development.

If or when the Threefoot Building finally gets the makeover it deserves, chances are good that the spirits that have lain dormant for so many years will be revived as well.

The Habitat for Humanity Office Building

The Habitat for Humanity Office is located at 1001 Twenty-ninth Avenue in a Meridian neighborhood known as the Redline District, which covers the northern part of Twenty-ninth Avenue. This neighborhood was named after the Red Line streetcar, which ran through the area. The site where the Habitat for Humanity Office is located was once occupied by a home owned by an African American woman—Missouri Larkin—and her husband. The legend of Missouri Larkin first appeared in the *Meridian Star* in 1918.

According to the reporter, Missouri Larkin and her husband owned a farm on Okatibbee Creek out on Highway 19, not far from Walmart. One day, Missouri did not come home from the farm. Her husband told the authorities that he did not know where she was. A few days after Missouri vanished, her ghost was seen in the Red Line area. Her spirit also appeared to a group of women who were working on a farm along Okatibbee Creek. She motioned the women to follow her, and when they did, they found her corpse floating in Okatibbee Creek. After Missouri's husband learned of the discovery of his wife's body, he left town and was never heard from again.

The building that now houses the Habitat for Humanity Office was constructed in 1928 as a Jitney Jungle. The room where Fonda Rush now has her office was the meat market. Chickens were butchered in the room that is

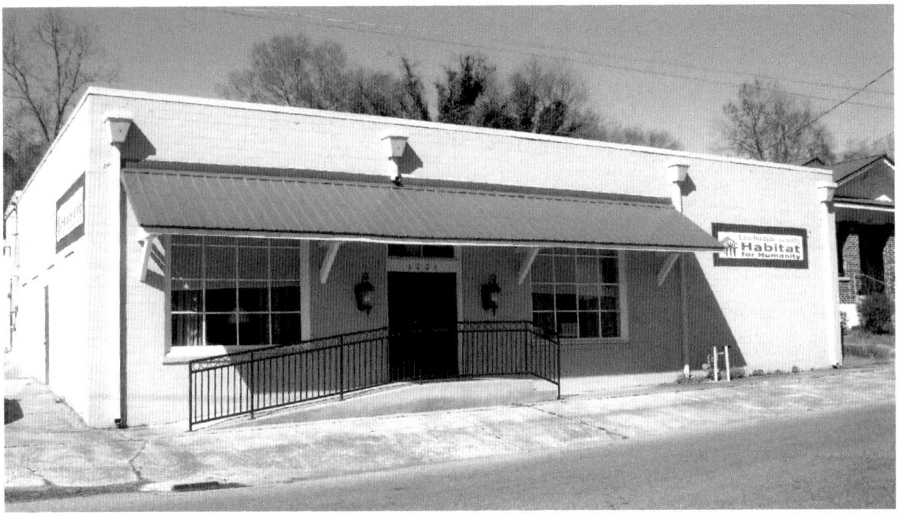

The Habitat for Humanity Office is housed in Meridian's first Jitney Jungle.

now the kitchen area. "When you came to the meat market in the 1920s, you really got fresh meat," Fonda said. When Habitat for Humanity took over the building, Fonda and another office worker, Mary Birge, soon realized that they were sharing their new offices with something otherworldly.

"Weird things would happen back then," Fonda said.

> *Mary's office was where our two bathrooms are now. She had a big window that is at the other end of the boardroom. She and I would both get up sometimes when the front door would open, and nobody was there. We used to have a little bell on the door—the bell had a little angel on it. The bell would usually ring when people came in, but sometimes, the bell rang when nobody was there. The toilet flushed on its own, too. We never saw anything. It just felt like people were there.*

In 2010, Fonda's secretary, Pat Hall, had a bizarre experience inside the Habitat Office. "I hear things all the time," Pat said,

> *like clicking sounds, footsteps. I hear the door open and close, too, like someone's coming in. Sometimes they do, and sometimes they don't. One day, I was sitting here at my desk, and a light in Fonda's office came on by itself. That really scared me. When Fonda came back to the office, I told here that I can't work in this building by myself.*

Many experts in the paranormal believe that children are more sensitive to spirits than adults are. An experience Fonda's grandson had in the Habitat Office when he was two years old would seem to support this theory. "We were remodeling and were getting ready for a house dedication," Fonda said.

> *On that particular day, my grandson was with me. We had brought over some things to put in the warehouse. My grandson—he was being potty-trained—said he wanted to go to the bathroom. I could see him through the side door here. When he came back, I had to change his clothes because he did not make it to the bathroom fast enough. Then we sat on the back steps. At the time, the door to the warehouse was open. My grandson kept looking behind me. Suddenly, he said, "Mamie, I don't like that man." At first, I thought someone had gotten in. I said, "What man?" He said that the man was standing behind me. "I like the littlte boy," he said, "but I don't like the man. The little boy wants to play with me, but the man scares me." I walked into the warehouse and looked around, and there was no one else in the building but us. I told him we needed to get back over to the Habitat House, so I picked him up, and we got in the truck and drove off. My grandson's mother said that he would talk about the boy and the man for several weeks after that experience. He doesn't say anything about it anymore. This is confirmation to me that there is something in this building.*

Fonda has never found out the identity of the ghosts haunting the Habitat for Humanity Office building. She suspects that the child could be the ghost of one of the children who died in Meridian's yellow fever epidemic. "The male ghost could be the ghost of Mr. Larkin," Fonda said. For the most part, though, Fonda is comfortable working in the former grocery store. She is so used to the paranormal activity that she and the other workers joke about it. "Sometimes, we blame all of the weird stuff that goes on around here on the ghosts of the chickens that ended up in the meat case."

HOOPER'S ELECTRONICS

Hooper's Electronics at 402 Twenty-second Avenue is housed in the old Hardin's Bakery building. Phil Hardin was an entrepreneur and marketing genius who took over the Meridian Baking Company in 1928 at Fifth Street and Thirtieth Avenue after it went bankrupt. In 1937, Phil Hardin built the then-state-of-the art bakery on Twenty-second Avenue. His new bakery had traveling proofers and traveling ovens. Every year, parents drove their children past the bakery to marvel at the animated figures of Santa Claus and his reindeer. The figures were made by David White, a longtime Hardin's employee.

In the 1950s, Phil Hardin sponsored a country music program on television station WTOK. The television show featured Danny and the Dudes playing "The Hardin's Bread Boogie." His bakeries also offered tours to elementary school children as part of Hardin's publicity campaign. By the 1960s, the Hardin Bakery Corporation was baking bread and rolls at its plants in Tupelo, Jackson and Meridian. The Hardin Bakery in Columbus produced sweet goods. In the 1970s, Hardin's management team closed the older plants around Mississippi and focused its attention on the state-of-the-art production and distribution center in Meridian. Eventually, Hardin's Bakery Corporation became the supplier for hamburger buns for McDonalds.

In 1964, Phil Hardin began thinking seriously about giving back to the community. After conferring with his business associate, Tom Ward, Hardin decided to start a foundation in his name. The first board of directors included his banker, his physician, his lawyer and three business associates.

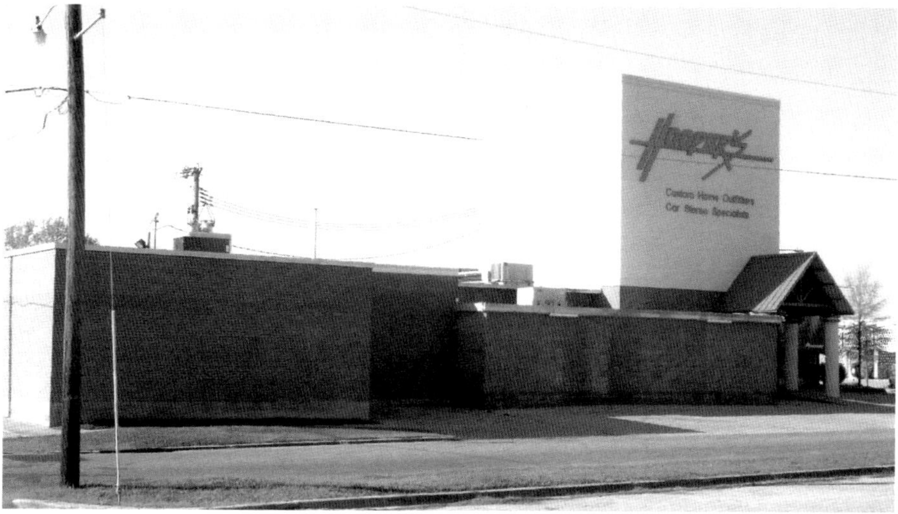

Hooper's Electronics.

Since Hardin's death in 1972, the Phil Hardin Foundation has awarded more than $3.8 million in grants and loans. Phil Hardin is still having an impact on the beneficiaries of his generosity and on the business that has moved into Hardin's Bakery.

Randy Hooper recalled what Hardin's Bakery looked like when he was a boy living in Meridian:

> *Hardin had started with the bakery building in the middle of the block. He then added the office building on to it. On the other end, they had a day-old bread sale retail place. The building itself was an actual bakery. When I was a kid, we toured the bakery in the early 1960s, and they gave us these little mini loaves of bread to eat. I was born in 1954, and I was in the second or third grade when this happened.*

Randy Hooper purchased the former bakery in the late 1970s. For the first eight or nine years, Randy used the building as a warehouse. He began to suspect that the former owner had not really left the building soon after he purchased the building. "At that time, it was not a retail store," Randy said.

> *It was a warehouse. We didn't do a whole lot to the building. We didn't make any structural changes in the building. I'd go down there at night and*

do catch-up work and stuff. I'd be sitting in Mr. Phil Hardin's old office, and I'd hear stuff. I'd hear footsteps going up and down the stairs to the second-floor offices. I'd hear doors close. It was a little scary. I was the only one down there, so I was the only one who heard these things. I told other people about it. I just kind of laughed about it. It wasn't like a mean ghost or ugly ghost. It was just a presence.

The only time Randy Hooper ever really felt scared in the building occurred one night in the early 1980s:

I was working there by myself when I heard a pretty loud noise in the main part of the warehouse. We had stacked a bunch of antennas on top of a surveillance platform that they had at the time. Later on, I figured out that it was these antennas that had fallen off the platform. It could have just as easily been a mouse or a critter or a rat that knocked them down, I suppose. I don't know what it was. I took my .45 and walked back through the warehouse, and something else made a noise in there that was pretty loud. I had my hand on the trigger, and I shot a hole in the floor. I told a couple of people about it. It was pretty embarrassing. It was the kind of thing you don't brag about. But it did teach me a couple of things about automatic weapons. They're probably more dangerous to the guy who's trying to protect himself.

After the retail store opened in the old bakery, Randy discovered that some vestiges of the building's past had not entirely faded away. "At one time, the bakery burned and was rebuilt, so I am assuming that the first bakery was primarily wood," Randy said.

When they rebuilt it, the center part of the structure had a lot of fill and concrete. It's a really heavily built building now. A sales rep for JVC walked through the building with me one time. He opened the door and said, "This building has been on fire before." He could smell that. I've never smelled it. There were no charred spots or anything. No one else has smelled the burned smell. He was a fireman before he was a sales rep.

Randy Hooper believes that Phil Hardin's connection to the bakery was so strong that it has transcended the grave. "Phil Hardin's life was the bakery," Randy said. "He didn't have any children. He spent all his time down there. Maybe he stayed on to see that something good would happen with this building."

Weidmann's Restaurant

For over a century, Weidmann's Restaurant has been an institution. The oldest continually operating business in Meridian, Mississippi, Weidmann's has survived the Riot of 1871, the yellow fever epidemic of 1878, the Tornado of 1906, the Great Depression, a devastating fire in 1958 and the Hurricane of 2004. For visitors arriving in Meridian by railroad or the Interstate, Weidmann's was the place to go for fine dining.

Photographs hanging from the walls provide customers with a sampling of the many celebrities who have eaten there: Ralph Bellamy, Primo Carnerea, Dizzy Dean, Jack Dempsey, Bob Feller, Spike Jones, Guy Lombardo, Tom Mix, Mary Ann Mobley, Marjorie Kinnan Rawlings, Dale Robertson, Babe Ruth and Gloria Vanderbilt. Film and television actress Sela Ward occasionally drops into Weidmann's whenever she returns to her hometown for a visit. Its fame has been so widespread that the *National Observer* called Weidmann's "the restaurant that made a city famous." Less well known are the spirits that have made Weidmann's their home.

When Weidmann's first opened for business in 1870, the city of 3,881 people was just recovering from the destructive effects of a massive fire in 1861 and General William Tecumseh Sherman's Valentine Day's visit in 1864. Its founder was Felix Weidmann, an immigrant from Zurich, Switzerland. However, in 2001, local historian Fonda Rush discovered proof in the *Meridian Gazette* that Felix's wife, Clara, actually started the establishment. Felix worked his way over to America as a chef on one of the big liners. Weidmann's Café originally consisted of a few stools and a

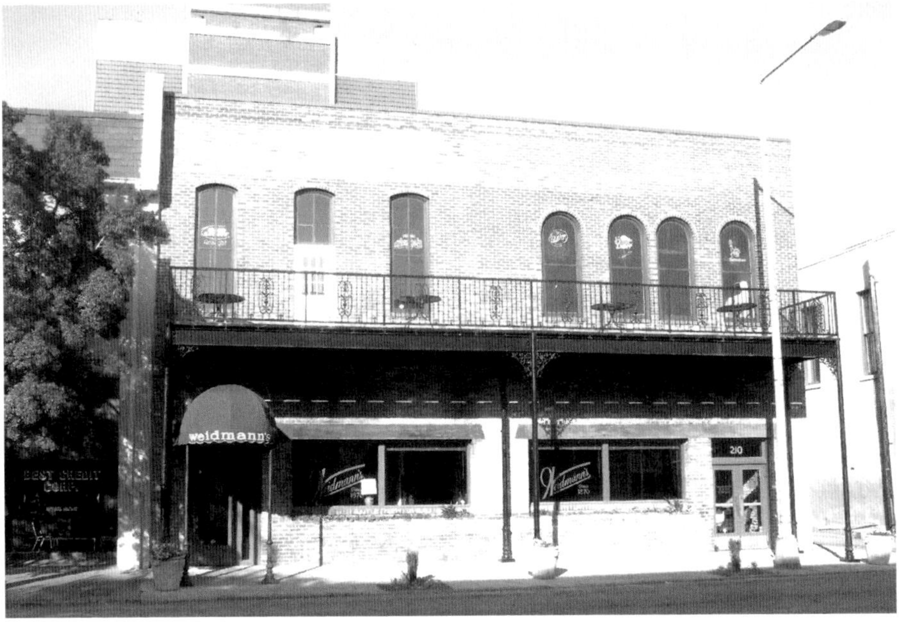

Weidmann's, Meridian's oldest restaurant.

counter. Felix built up his clientele by making fresh chocolate éclairs every afternoon to serve with hot Niolon's coffee.

One of Felix's four sons, Phillip, became the owner of the restaurant in 1901. "The Restaurant," as it became known locally for many years, moved around in its early days to several downtown locations before Phillip moved it to its present location on Twenty-second Avenue in 1923. Phillip's specialties were garlic-boiled shrimp and oyster loaves consisting of a loaf of unsliced bread filled with a dozen or two fried oysters, celery, pickles and catsup.

After Phillip Weidmann died in 1927, his only son, Henry, took over the family restaurant. Henry, a gourmet chef, is generally credited with turning his grandfather's four-stool café into one of the best restaurants in the South. He created Weidmann's best-known dessert: black-bottom pie. According to a brochure written by Henry's daughter, Mary, "Daddy was like a Ring Circus Master in the midst of a big circus act—or an orchestra conductor—when he was 'on stage' at the Restaurant. He knew every detail—every nook and crook of every room. He had a very sensitive nature, and an artistic touch."

To accommodate the railroad men who worked odd hours, Henry kept the restaurant open twenty-four hours a day, a policy that remained in place until Henry's death in 1926. In the 1940s, a neon sign proclaiming, "Through these doors walk the finest people on earth—our customers" hung over the door. One of the best-known stories about Henry's love for his customers took place during World War II. Henry had given his employees the day off on Christmas Day. Looking out from his apartment above the restaurant, Henry saw two sailors looking through the windows. He opened the restaurant and cooked Christmas dinner for the two servicemen. Another story concerns the origin of the peanut butter crocks, which became a fixture at Weidmann's for sixty years. Because butter was rationed during World War II, Henry began offering his customers peanut butter and crackers as appetizers.

Following the death of Henry Weidmann in 1956, his son-in-law, T.E. "Shorty" McWilliams, took over the management of the restaurant. Shorty, a professional football player who made all-American three times while at Mississippi State University, had worked with Henry for eight years prior to the older man's death. Weidmann's was partially destroyed by fire in 1958, but Shorty and his mother-in-law, Dorothy, rebuilt it. Shorty also added two dining rooms, increasing Weidmann's seating capacity to 325.

In 1984, Henry Weidmann's granddaughter, Gloria Chancellor, became the fifth generation of the Weidmann family to run the restaurant. She and her husband, Poo Chancellor, served lunch for the last time on October 4, 2001, when Weidmann's was sold to a group of investors called the Weidmann's Square Group, headed up by local businessmen Fred Wile, Bruce Martin and Miles Frank. Weidmann's was closed for renovations, and many of the furnishings, including the peanut butter jars and the plates, were auctioned off. When Weidmann's reopened almost a year later as Weidmann's Square, about the only things left from the original restaurant were a couple of light fixtures now hanging in the bar and many of the old photographs, which adorn the wall near the entrance and upstairs bar. A sole peanut butter jar displayed on the wall is a nostalgic reminder of the Weidmann's that used to be.

Weidmann's closed on April 27, 2010, but in June of that same year, Charles Frazier, former manager of Crescent City Grill, purchased the lease to the building. He made several structural changes to the restaurant before it reopened a month later, including restoring the lunch counter, removing the back wall and installing hardwood floors. Even customers who remember the Weidmann's of yesteryear seem satisfied with the restaurant in its new incarnation, primarily because the food and the service are just as good as they have always been.

Less tangible remnants of the past are the ghost stories that have been passed down by employees and customers for decades. One of the best-developed stories involves Adam and Sarah Jane, a young couple from north Mississippi. One day during the Great Depression, they were traveling through the state on a job-hunting search that, if successful, would enable them to get money. With money they had earned doing odd jobs, they decided to treat themselves to a good meal at Weidmann's. When the waiter brought the check, Henry Weidmann picked it up and told the young couple, "Dinner is our engagement gift to you." Adam replied, "We'll be back to celebrate our first anniversary." Adam and Sarah Jane never returned.

Writing in the October 30, 2001 edition of the *Meridian Star*, Katherine Horne speculates:

> *Rumors ran that she died of polio, others that he was killed in the war. But on a certain date, some say, late at night; you may glimpse in a quickly fading vignette against a wall near the fireplace an aura as softly yellow as candlelight over Sarah Jane and Adam, who sit holding hands under the table.*

To this day, staff at the restaurant still claim to see the ghosts of the young lovers at table number one.

Other ghost stories center on the staff of the restaurant. Mary McLaughlin, a student at Meridian Community College, worked at Weidmann's between 1993 and 1994 as a cashier and hostess. When she first started working there, she began hearing stories from the wait staff concerning a spectral voice:

> *Several people told me that when you least expect it, you might hear your name called. You're busy doing something, and all of a sudden, someone calls your name. I heard it the first time after I had been working there for a few weeks. Both times, I heard it when I least expected it. I'd be answering the phone or writing something down. It always happened to me in the day, never at night. I couldn't figure out if it was a male or female voice.*

Curiosity drove Mary to talk to the other employees at the restaurant, and she discovered that everyone who had worked there for at least a month had the same experience. She also found out that the voice was heard everywhere in the restaurant. One afternoon, Mary was talking to a waitress named Diane, and all of a sudden, Diane said, "It happened again! They just called my name!"

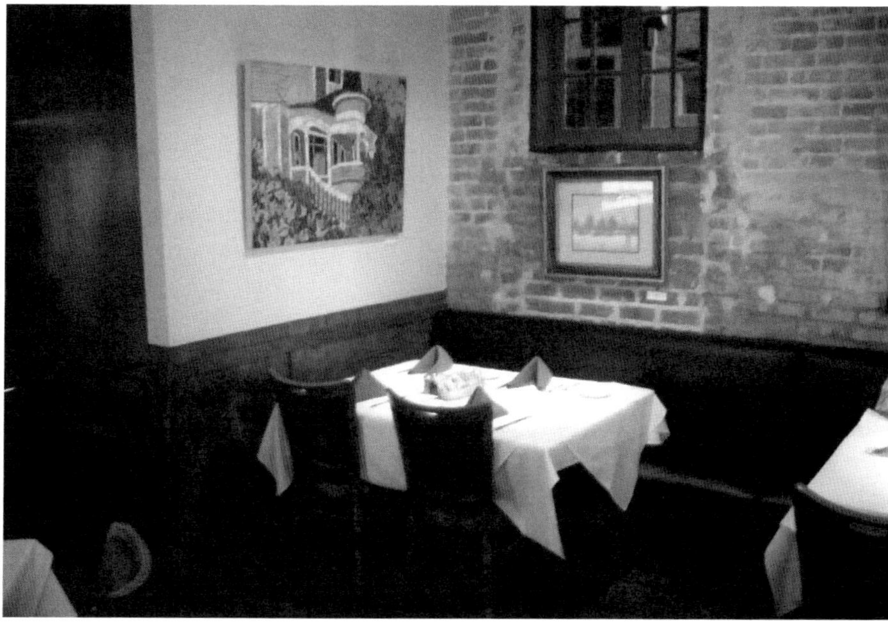

The ghosts of a young couple still celebrate their wedding anniversary at table number one in Weidmann's.

Mary's second encounter with the spirits of Weidmann's took place one night around closing time. Mary was counting up the money, and the hostess was making sure all the doors were locked in the back and in the kitchen and that all the lights were off. Just as the hostess was on her way to the kitchen, something very strange happened. "All of a sudden, the doors that go from the dining room into the kitchen burst open, like somebody was walking through really fast," Mary said.

> *At first, I thought it was her* [the hostess] *going in the back. I didn't think twice about it. Then—Boom! This time, the doors flew open again in the opposite direction. It was like someone had come out of the main dining room into the kitchen. I yelled her name, but she was already upstairs. There's no way she could have gone downstairs and come back upstairs in a few seconds.*

She mentioned the incident to Shorty McWilliams afterward. "He didn't say anything. He just gave me a little mischievous smile, like he knew what I was talking about."

A different hostess had an unnerving experience in the 1870 Room late one night around closing time:

> *She was waiting for the cashier to finish up when all of a sudden, she heard this huge crash in the 1870 Room, which is basically one big, wide-open space. It doesn't have any doors. She said it was so loud that you could hear the ground shake. She flipped on the light switch to see what was broken. Nothing had fallen on the floor. She then looked over at the little mini bar. There was no glass on the floor whatsoever.*

Mary McLaughlin, who was also working that night, ran into the 1870 Room, thinking that the old grandfather clock had fallen over. She was shocked to find that nothing had been disturbed. The next day, a waiter named Willy who had worked at Weidmann's for fifty years overheard Mary and the hostess talking about the mysterious crash. He walked over to the two women and said:

> *You know that big steamboat wheel chandelier came crashing down one night years ago in the same season that we are in now. It was really heavy. We had a storm that night, and the thunder could have shaken it loose from the ceiling. I came in the next morning, and pieces of it were all over the floor.*

The crashing chandelier bears all the earmarks of a residual haunting. In *The Ghost Hunter's Guidebook*, author Troy Taylor explains, "Many of the locations where these hauntings take place experience an event (or a series of events) that imprints itself on the atmosphere of the place. This event can suddenly discharge and play itself at various times, just as a recording would."

The only longtime employee, other than Willy, who would talk to Mary about the paranormal activity at the restaurant was Shorty McWilliams. "Poo and Gloria didn't want us to talk about the ghosts," Mary said. "They weren't real strict about it, though. Shorty, though, didn't care if the customers knew about the ghosts or not." Shorty told Mary that sometimes he heard noises coming from the kitchen:

> *In the back of the kitchen area where the freezer is now, they used to keep livestock. This would have been in the 1910s–1920s. Shorty told me that every once in a while when you don't expect it, you might hear something that doesn't sound quite normal, like a "moo" from a cow or the sound of an animal bumping against the walls.*

Shorty told Mary that the best time to hear strange noises in the restaurant is at night. Occasionally, he heard footsteps coming from the upper floor when no one else was in the building. Mary said that beginning in the 1950s, the upstairs was a special dining area called the Downtown Club:

> *Henry made it into a special place for local business owners, bank presidents and lawyers to have lunch. They paid monthly dues and had their own key to a special door. The Downtown Club had a bar, a waitress and a waiter. I was up there once, and it was beautifully decorated with stained glass and brass.*

Shorty told Mary that late at night, he heard people walking up the stairs leading from the original door to the Downtown Club. "He said he just got used to hearing it."

Weidmann's looks different after it reopened in 2010, but one feature of the restaurant that has not changed is the ghost stories that employees still tell about the old place. One evening, a policeman who was passing by Weidmann's noticed that the door to the old Downtown Club above Weidmann's was ajar. When he tried to shut the door, it felt like someone was pushing against it on the other side. Some employees have heard spectral voices and ghostly laughter in different parts of the old restaurant.

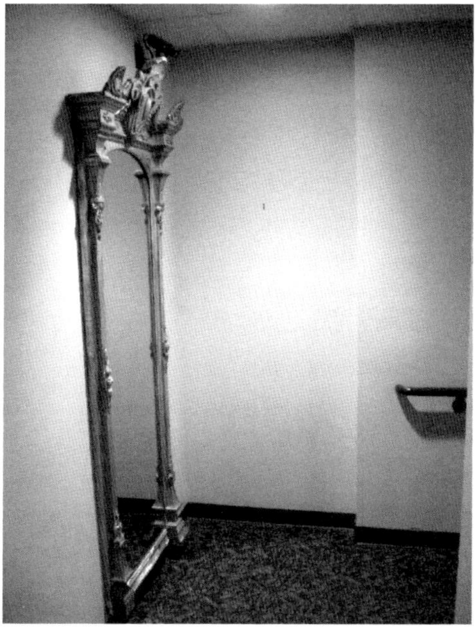

Spectral faces have been seen in the mirror on the second floor of Weidmann's.

A greeter named Carrie, who has worked at Weidmann's since October 2010, told me in December 2010 that she had had a number of strange experiences in the restaurant during the short time she had been working there. She answered the telephone only to find that there was no one on the line. She also said that several times when she was walking up the stairs to the second floor, she saw shadowy figures out of the corner of her eye standing by the mirror on the landing.

Weidmann's has come a long way since the 1870s, when such people as the coffee man, the vegetable lady, the fish man and the German lady who made fresh cream cheese and sour cream visited the restaurant daily. Many travelers, passing close to Meridian, still make a special effort to go to Weidmann's, just as people did more than a century ago. The interior might have changed, but the time-honored tradition of fine food and Mississippi hospitality continues at the old restaurant. If the servers, cooks and greeters at Weidmann's are to be believed, some ghostly fragments of the past are still there as well.

The Pigford Building

In 1915, a three-story, red brick building was constructed at 820 Twenty-second Street by Mount Barton Lodge No. 13, Knights of Pythias. Originally known as Pythian Castle Hall, the lodge provided club rooms and meeting space for its members. In the 1920s, Pigford Realty purchased the building. The first floor was rented out to a variety of different stores. Offices were housed on the second floor. A lavish ballroom occupied the third floor. Between 1933 and 1976, R.M. Hamil operated a post office/drugstore on the first floor. In 2000, the upper two floors of the Pigford Building were closed. By this time, the first floor was just beginning to acquire a reputation for being haunted.

In the early 1990s, a woman (who prefers to remain anonymous) opened a graphic design business in the Pigford Building. Not long after she opened, the owner and her employers began having strange experiences inside the building. People began hearing whimpering sounds at the same time every day. Several times, the owner returned to her office in the morning and found that everything on her desk had been rearranged. She also heard footsteps on the second floor when she was the only one in the store. One night, the owner's three-year-old cousin, who had been spending the day with her, came down from the mezzanine and said, "I don't like the lady in the long dress, and she doesn't like me." One night, the owner's young daughter heard a voice speaking to her over the intercom. Thinking that it was her mother, she said, "What is it, Mom?" To the child's surprise, her mother had not used the intercom at all that night.

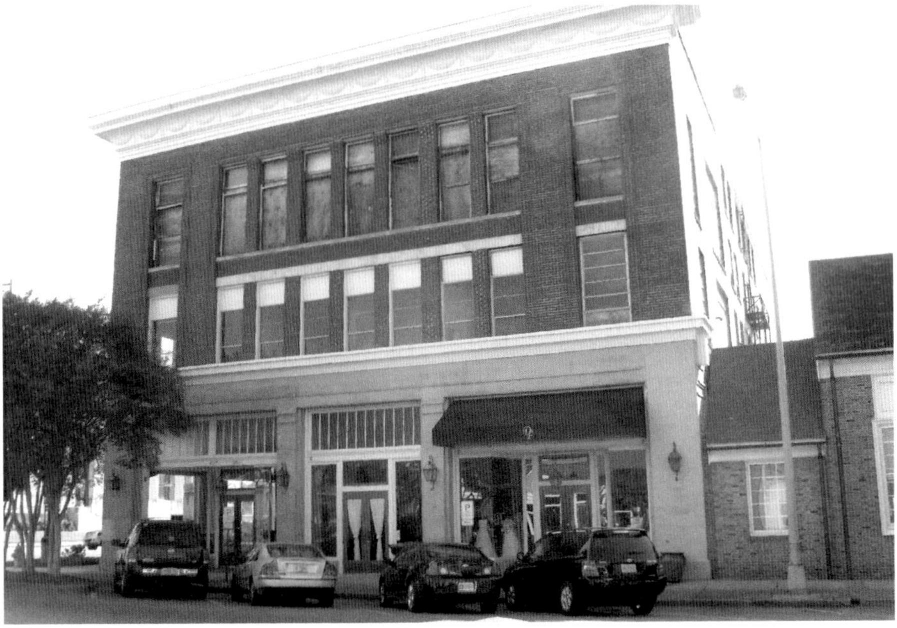

Several businesses housed inside the Pigford Building have reported high levels of paranormal activity over the years.

Sometimes the owner was overcome by an uncomfortable feeling, as if some invisible entity were hovering around her. "You could feel her when she walked in the room," she said. "I would be sitting there drawing at night, and you'd feel like this warm thing." Despite the fact that most people experienced fear when encountering the female spirit, the owner only felt pity for her. "She was really sad," she said. "I could be down there by myself, and I did not feel endangered. She was hurt, and you could tell she was hurt."

In October 1999, a clothing and gift shop called Alexander's opened its doors on the first floor. Almost immediately, customers and employees began having strange experiences inside the store. A month later, people began spreading rumors about hearing spectral laughter inside the store. The paranormal activity escalated over the next few weeks. Employees who opened the store in the morning began finding clothes that had been hung up the night before scattered all over the floor. On May 15, 1999, an employee named J.T. Mohammad was standing on the first floor when she happened to look up. She was shocked to see a white woman wearing a handkerchief-like dress floating across the balcony. Afterward, Mohammad described the woman as having long hair. She also seemed to glow. Oddly enough, Mohammad was not really frightened by the ghost.

That same year, one of the owners of the store had a much more terrifying experience inside Alexander's. She was sitting in a little office room after-hours counting money when the telephone rang. At the time, the store had one phone line for inside calls and another line for outside calls. She thought it was odd that she was receiving a phone call from an inside line because she was alone in the store at the time. Her flesh began to crawl when she said, "Hello" and heard nothing but heavy breathing on the line. Thinking that another employee was trying to scare her, the woman walked through the store in search of the prankster. When she was satisfied that no one else was in the store, she returned to her office. A few minutes later, the inside phone rang again. When she answered the phone and heard the same strange sounds, the woman decided that it was time to go home.

The next year, a reporter from the *Meridian Star* next door, Marianne Todd, had her own frightening encounter in Alexander's. She walked into the store about twenty minutes before closing time, picked out several dresses and blouses and began trying them on in one of the dressing rooms. Suddenly, she heard noises coming from the dressing room next to hers. Marianne thought that she and the clerk were the only ones in the store, but her curiosity overcame her fear, and she opened the door to the dressing room. As soon as she discovered that the dressing room was empty, Marianne dropped the clothes she was trying on and rushed out the front door.

On October 30, 1999, two disc jockeys from local radio station WOKK—Scotty Ray Boyd and Debbie Alexander—spent the night at Alexander's to see if there was any truth to the stories that had been circulating around Meridian for several months. The disc jockeys were accompanied by several guests. Debbie fell asleep after a few hours, but Scotty Ray was kept awake by things that he saw and heard, beginning at 9:00 p.m. He and several of the guests noticed an office chair moving back and forth. They also said that clothes hanging on a rack began swinging as if someone walking down the aisle had brushed against them. Scotty Ray took these strange occurrences in stride—until he discovered that he could not open the door to the roof. He and a technician had gone through that door several times that evening in order to run cables through the building. Scotty Ray's belief that Alexander's was haunted was substantiated the next morning when Debbie found a pair of earrings lying beside her. "If somebody rigged all this stuff up this way to scare us, they did a pretty good job because it all seemed real to me," Scotty Ray said.

On October 23, 2008, I—accompanied by *Meridian Star* reporter Jennifer Jacob, *Meridian Star* photographer Paula Merritt and librarian Kevin Chatham—conducted a paranormal investigation of the Dream It dress shop, which now occupies the same space as Alexander's. When we arrived at 8:30 p.m., the owner, Theresa Long, told us about the strange experiences that she and others have had in the old building. Theresa said that her son has seen objects move by themselves on the mezzanine. He has also had the feeling of being watched up there. On two separate occasions, she and her daughter, Monica, saw the vacuum cleaner, which had been unplugged, turn back on by itself. Theresa also heard footsteps on the upper floor at a time when her shop was the only store in the building. She has even seen the floorboards on the upper floor give way, as if someone—or something—were walking on them. Theresa said that electronic devices, like her radio and her computer, malfunction all the time. The batteries in one of the clocks tend to run low constantly.

At 9:00 p.m., we began taking photographs all over the building. A half hour later, all of us gathered around a table on the second floor and conducted an EVP session. After a few minutes, Theresa said that she began feeling cold. Using an infrared thermometer, I found that the temperature around Theresa was seventy-six degrees, but the temperature in the rest of the room was eighty-two degrees. Theresa experienced several drops in temperature over the course of the evening. Later, we discovered that several electronic devices had been acting strangely during our EVP session. Theresa's computer shut down on its own for the first time since she bought it. The clock that seemed to drain batteries gained two minutes. An alarm system, which had not worked since the store opened, suddenly turned on all by itself. Unfortunately, no corroborating evidence was captured by our cameras or our voice recorders.

Our investigation did not prove beyond a doubt that the Pigford Building was haunted. However, any paranormal investigator knows that ghosts do not perform on cue. Too many bizarre occurrences have been reported over the years by sober, sensible people to dismiss their sightings as nothing more than figments of the imagination.

The Meridian Public Library

The Meridian Public Library lacks the Victorian veneer that many of the nation's more famous haunted libraries have. Built in 1967, the library was a rather ordinary-looking, boxlike, yellow brick structure, a popular style for civic buildings constructed in the South in the late 1960s. It was located on the corner of Twenty-sixth Avenue and Seventh Street on the site of the A.J. Lyons Home, which was constructed in 1906 at the cost of $6,000. In 1942, the house was occupied by the USO Club after extensive renovations. The Lyons Home was torn down to make room for the library in 1967. Mrs. Lyons's real home might be gone, but some say that her ghost has taken up residence in the library, along with the spirit of a former librarian.

Librarians who have encountered the ghost haunting the Meridian Public Library claim that it manifests itself not as a full-bodied apparition but in the form of sounds and eerie feelings. Librarian Kevin Chatham and library director Steven McCartney have both heard strange noises and experienced cold spots on the second floor. McCartney says:

> *Most of the cold spots on the second floor have been detected in the room where we keep the book sale books. This is not a public area. The other place where I have felt cold spots is in my office, which is kind of frightening. Only small areas in my office have been unusually cold. I'll sit here and feel cold, and other people have come into my office and sat in front of my desk, and they didn't feel cold at all. Most of the time, the temperature in my office is pretty constant. The chills are usually accompanied by a feeling*

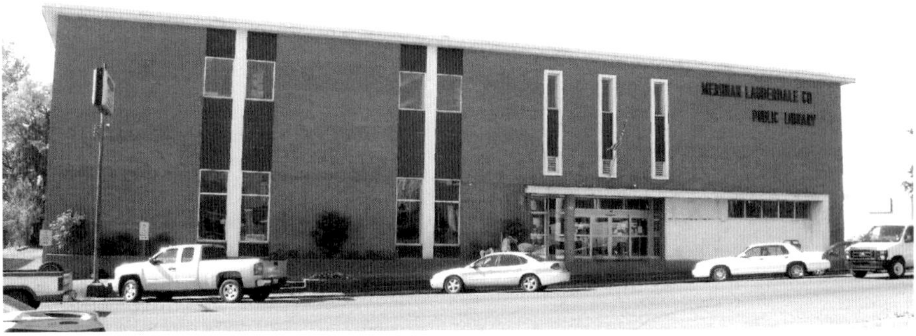

The Meridian Public Library.

> *of unease. Whether it's a natural phenomenon or something else, I don't know. I have felt the cold spots between four and six times.*

Other staff members working upstairs have felt uneasy in the processing area and around a particular storage closet.

The elevator also seems to be very haunted. One night, McCartney was working late by himself. He distinctly remembers locking all the doors and turning off the lights. McCartney was working in his office off to the side of the mezzanine when he heard the elevator ding, signaling that someone was about to get off on his floor. Picking up his flashlight, McCartney walked through the library in search of an intruder, but no one was there. "The elevator went down to the first floor on one occasion. Another time, it went to the basement. There was nobody else in the building. Just me. The last time this happened was in 2007. That elevator's strange," he said. Kevin Chatham said that sometimes when he takes the elevator to the second floor, he is overcome with what he describes as a "heavy feeling."

Most of the librarians who have encountered the ghost believe that it is female. Two possibilities have been offered as to the identity of the spirit. One of these is that it is the ghost of Mrs. A.J. Lyons—Josephine—who committed suicide in her home. However, most of the library staff believe that the library is being haunted by head librarian Jeanne Broach.

Born in Meridian in April 1913, Ms. Broach graduated from Meridian High School in 1930. She received her bachelor's degree from the Mississippi State College for Women in 1934 and her master's in English from the University of Alabama in 1935. Following a stint in the U.S. Naval Reserve between 1942 and 1945, Ms. Broach became head librarian at Meridian Public Library. She is remembered as a stern woman with big glasses who stood up on the mezzanine and watched her employees down below. Ms. Broach loved efficiency as much as she loved books, and the staff knew it. She retired on October 31, 1975, and died on October 19, 1976. In an article published in the *Meridian Star* on November 6, 1976, the writer, Maureen Christian, described Ms. Broach as a "no-nonsense" woman who opposed having the library renamed in her honor because doing so would be a waste of time. Those who knew Ms. Broach recall her saying more than once that people should "let the past go." It would be ironic indeed if her ghost were the spirit that walks the halls of the Meridian Public Library.

Steve McCartney believes that the ghost of Jeanne Broach is haunting the library:

> *After working here for twenty years, I am convinced that Miss Jeanne Broach is still here in some form or fashion. If the power was out and it was the middle of the night, I wouldn't want to go in the room where Ms. Broach's portrait hangs.*

In fact, he is certain that Ms. Broach's ghost is responsible for the cold spots in his office, possibly because her spirit is strongly attached to the furnishings. "Everything in this office, with the exception of the file cabinet and the television set, was here in Ms. Broach's time," McCartney said. "Sometimes, I look at her portrait, and I wonder if the old girl's still around."

According to Steve McCartney, some of the library's visitors detected an evil entity in the library:

> *A group of people were talking to me in my office for about ten minutes. Then they left and walked down the stairs. All of a sudden, they were back in the doorway. One of the women said, "We were standing at the bottom of the stairs, and I was overcome with a sense of evil."*

McCartney does not believe that the woman was sensing the presence of Ms. Broach. "She might have been a stern taskmaster, but she was basically a good person, from what I've heard," McCartney said. "I think that the psychic lady was sensing evil in one of the library's patrons, who might have been standing by the stairs at the time."

In the fall of 2008, a janitor named Nick had a terrifying experience in the library. One Saturday morning, he was cleaning up in the library between

6:30 and 7:30 a.m. At the time, he was the only person in the library. He went to the break room on the second floor and was sitting in a chair when he heard a woman's voice call his name. Nick searched all over the second floor, but no one besides him was there. Afterward, he told Kevin Chatham that prior to this incident, he had heard other strange noises in the library, like the sound of books being shelved. To keep from hearing unnerving noises, Nick now turns on the television in the break room when he is alone in the library.

On October 16, 2008, *Meridian Star* reporter Jennifer Jacobs, *Meridian Star* photographer Paula Merritt, librarian Kevin Chatham, Cory Brown and I conducted a paranormal investigation of the Meridian Public Library. At 9:00 p.m., we arrived at the library, which was closed to the general public. Armed with digital cameras, video cameras, voice recorders, EMF meters and infrared thermometers, we walked through the entire building, beginning at the basement and ending on the second floor. We focused most of our attention on those areas where staff members have felt uncomfortable. When we were in the basement, we turned out the lights and began collecting EVPs. Ten minutes after we began, I asked the spirit to give us a sign of its presence. A few second later, we heard a strange clicking noise. Other members began asking similar questions, and once again, something clicked. When we turned on the lights, we began searching for the source of the sound. I must admit that we were disappointed when we traced the noise to a fuse box, which clicked periodically. We were also able to explain away other "spectral" sounds that we heard during the remainder of the evening, such as the ticking of a clock.

The only incident for which we could not provide a logical explanation occurred in the processing room at about 11:30 p.m. We were seated around a table conducting one final EVP session when Paula Merritt asked if she was the only one in the room who was feeling cold. Every person in the room agreed that the temperature seemed to have dropped. Using my infrared thermometer, I checked the temperature and was surprised to find that it had not dropped at all. A few minutes later, Paula said that she felt something brush against her cheek. No insects appeared to be in the room at the time.

Toward the end of the investigation, we were sitting at a table on the first floor, collecting EVPs. Suddenly, Kevin asked me, "Did you hear a baby crying?" I told him that I did not hear anything at all. The next day, Kevin mentioned the crying to another librarian named Rhonda. She said that she had heard the baby's cries several times. A few days later, during my book signing at the library, former librarian Sarah Mutziger said that she had also heard a baby crying once when she was in the library all by herself.

Even though the investigation of the Meridian Public Library produced no hard evidence of a haunting, the personal experiences of the staff cannot be discounted. According to experts in the paranormal, women like Mrs. Lyons and Ms. Broach frequently become restless spirits after death. Many buildings are reputed to be haunted by the ghosts of people who are trapped at the place where they took their own lives. Librarians, most of whom are very dedicated individuals, find it difficult to leave the jobs that meant so much to them. Regardless of who the ghost is, the Meridian Public Library will probably be a very "unquiet" place for some time.

THE GYPSY QUEEN'S GRAVE (ROSE HILL CEMETERY)

Meridian has been known as the "Queen City" for almost a century, but no one really knows why. Some people believe that the city's name dates back to the late nineteenth and early twentieth centuries, when Meridian was an important stop for the Queen and Crescent, a passenger train running between Cincinnati and New Orleans. In 1883, Meridian served as an exchange point for engines when the Queen and Crescent raced the Louisville & Nashville's fastest passenger train from Cincinnati to New Orleans.

However, many residents cling to the more romantic explanation for the city's royal name: that Meridian is named after Kelly Mitchell, queen of the gypsies. In 1915, Kelly Mitchell was brought to Meridian from a gypsy camp near Coatopa, Alabama, by her husband Emil, king of the gypsies. She was suffering from complications resulting from the birth of her fifteenth child. Emil offered the physician treating his wife $10,000 if he could save her life. Unfortunately, the doctor was unable to save her. Kelly Mitchell died on January 31, 1915, at the age of forty-seven.

The gypsy queen's relatives and followers decided to bury her in Meridian because it was the nearest city with enough ice to preserve her corpse until the time of the funeral. Her corpse was delivered to Watkins Funeral Home, where it was stored for six weeks while her family informed other bands of gypsies regarding the location and date of the funeral. Four bands of gypsies, consisting of the Mitchell, Marks, Bimbo and Costello families, eventually made their way to Mississippi for the funeral. Walton W. Moore, caretaker

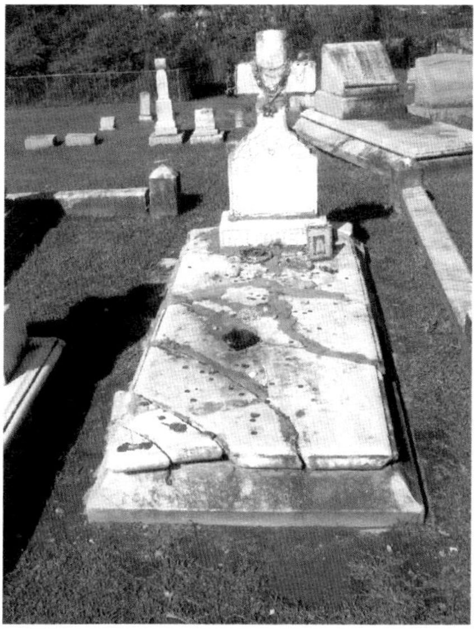

The grave of Kelly Mitchell, the last queen of the gypsies, in Rose Hill Cemetery.

of Rose Hill Cemetery, said that just before the funeral, gypsies were camped all over Meridian in parks and schools and on church lawns. Music for the funeral procession was provided by the Beeson College band. The band members were told by the gypsies: "Snap it up. It's a party."

Over twenty thousand people viewed the gypsy queen's body as it lay in state at the Horace C. Smith Undertaking Company. According to an article that appeared in the 1915 edition of the *Meridian Dispatch*, Kelly Mitchell was "attired in a robe of royal gypsy green and other bright colors. Two necklaces are around the neck, one composed of golden coins and the other of shells." Local resident Kline Shank said that jeweled combs had been placed in her hair. The services were said to be those of the Episcopal Church. Not long after the gypsy queen was interred in Meridian's Rose Hill Cemetery, locals began spreading rumors about her extravagant send-off. She was said to have been buried in a gold- or silver-lined mahogany casket worth $15,000. However, records show that no coffin worth more than $150 was bought in Meridian the year of Kelly Mitchell's funeral. The top of her glistening coffin was covered in glass. Her followers were reputed to have filled her casket with coins and jewelry that would be worth over $900,000 today. However, Kline Shank recalled seeing only a few coins that the gypsy queen's children had dropped inside the coffin. He also said that a change of clothing and silver coins were placed around Kelly Mitchell's corpse just before the casket was sealed.

These fantastic tales about Kelly Mitchell's lavish coffin inspired a number of would-be grave robbers to excavate her casket. Large cracks—evidence of a grave robbery gone awry—crisscross the marble, or wolf stone, covering her grave. A more industrious thief even tried to dig a tunnel to her coffin through the side of the hill where she is buried. Ironically, the pennies, nickels and dimes that the Mitchell family tossed in Kelly Mitchell's coffin probably did not amount to more than fifty dollars. To prevent her grave from being desecrated even further, Kelly Mitchell's family placed her casket in a steel vault, which was then covered in concrete.

Emil Mitchell was buried next to his wife following his death on October 16, 1942, at the age of eighty-five in Albertville, Alabama. He was buried in street clothes in a gray coffin. Relatives tossed coins in his coffin, just as they had done for his wife. He was also given several changes of clothes for his long journey to the afterlife. His nephew, Mike Wilson Mitchell, was killed in a car crash while driving to Emil's funeral and was buried alongside his uncle. Several other members of the Mitchell family are interred at the same site, including Joe Sharkie Mitchell. Next to his tombstone is a Schiltz beer can carved in stone.

Today, the graves of Kelly and Emil Mitchell are considered one of the main Romani burial grounds in the Southeast. Gypsies travel hundreds of miles to pay tribute to the king and queen of the gypsies, often leaving little tributes at the grave site—such as Mardi Gras beads, cigarettes and coins—in the belief that leaving an offering will entice the gypsy queen's spirit to visit them and to answer their problems. Occasionally, Orange Crush cans show up Kelly Mitchell's grave because that was her favorite soft drink. One day, cemetery caretaker Walton Moore found coconut cake, half consumed by ants, on top of Kelly Mitchell's grave.

Interestingly enough, most of the objects placed on the graves remain there, primarily because of a gypsy curse that is said to have been placed over the Mitchells' graves. According to Walton Moore, the curse did not deter one woman living near the cemetery. For years, she visited the Mitchells' grave site each week and scooped up the pennies, nickels, dimes and quarters into an old coffee can.

It is also possible that the gypsy queen herself is guarding her grave. In the early 2000s, a woman who was photographing several of the graves close to the entrance saw a female apparition in white float very slowly from the northeast corner of the cemetery. Before the photographer could scream, the semitransparent figure faded away. The photographer left Rose Hill Cemetery convinced that she had encountered the ghost of Kelly Mitchell. However, even if the woman did see an apparition in the old cemetery, chances are good that it could have been the spirit of one of the hundreds of other women who are buried there.

THE *MERIDIAN STAR*

The *Meridian Star*, located at 814 Twenty-second Avenue, has been the city's only daily newspaper since 1921. The newspaper started out as the *Evening Star* in 1898 but changed its name in 1915. The *Meridian Star*, with a circulation of approximately twelve thousand, serves subscribers in western Alabama and eastern Mississippi. The *Meridian Star* is like any other newspaper office in that on most days it is engulfed in a flurry of activity. According to some past and present employees, some of that activity is paranormal.

Today, the *Meridian Star* occupies almost an entire block. In the 1920s, however, an alley separated the newspaper office from the Pigford Building next door. Housed in the back part of the building, facing Twenty-first Avenue, was an old car dealership. The showroom was located in what is now the glass-enclosed section of the *Meridian Star*. What is now the pressroom used to be the shop. According to local lore, two men died in or around this building. One man was crushed under the hydraulic lift in the shop, and another died after falling into the alley from a second-story floor in the Pigford Building. These two incidents are believed to have produced the ghosts that still haunt the *Meridian Star* building to this day.

Most of the earliest tales of hauntings in the *Meridian Star* building began in the 1990s. One of these stories involved the former sports editor, Jeff Christina, who said that he and a woman named Rosalind were working late one night when they developed a craving for popcorn. Rosalind walked down the hallway to the break room and proceeded to microwave a bag of

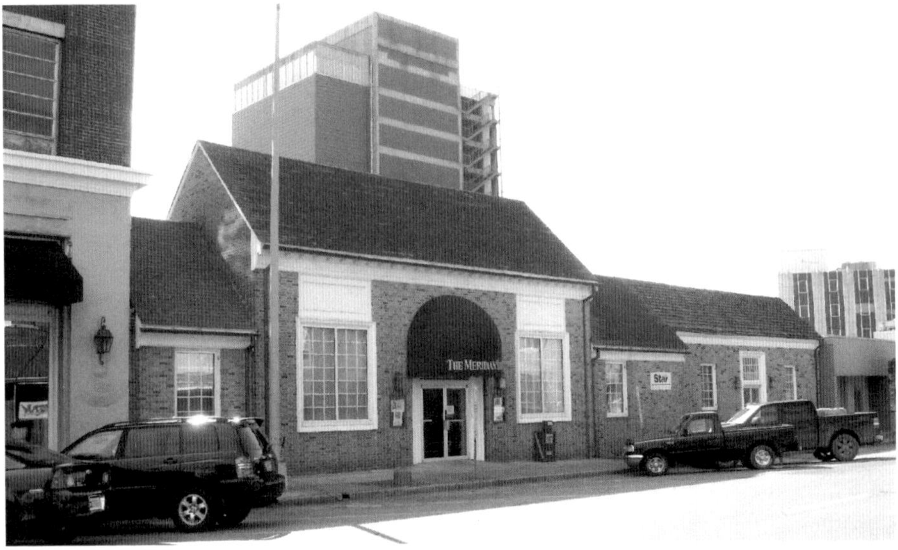

The *Meridian Star* office.

popcorn. When Rosalind returned, Jeff could tell by the stricken look on her face that something was wrong. She said that she was walking down the long hallway through the old part of the building when she saw a very small child, between two and three years old, dart across the entrance to one of the rooms. Her first thought was that one of the employees had brought the child to work and inadvertently left him or her there. She dashed into the room, expecting to find the child, but it was entirely empty. Rosalind said she combed the entire building but found no trace of the child.

The majority of the sightings in the *Meridian Star* building have occurred in the staff room. Just a few weeks after Rosalind's encounter, Jeff was working late all by himself in the pressroom. At 2:00 a.m., he was walking between the double doors of the pressroom and the newsroom when he passed through a cold spot. He happened to gaze up toward the ceiling and saw what he later described as two "bowling pin–shaped figures" floating over the pipes that ran along the upper wall. The white, amorphous entities appeared to be approximately seven or eight feet tall. After hovering over Jeff's head for a few seconds, the ghosts flew up into the ceiling and vanished. Not long thereafter, reporter Marianne Todd saw the same apparitions. She said that the two specters intertwined before zipping up into the ceiling.

Staff photographer Paula Merritt had an entirely different experience in the dark room late one afternoon in October 2000. Paula said that she had shut the door and was placing the film she had just shot in a canister containing the developing fluid when a bright light flashed across the room. Afterward, she described the light as being streaked with the kinds of rays that appear when a watch crystal reflects light against a wall. Even though the room was plunged back into darkness after a couple of seconds, Paula's heart sank because she was certain that the light had lasted long enough to ruin her film. She threw the rest of the film into the canister in the hope that she would be able to salvage at least one or two images. Paula then checked the door to see if it was tightly shut and examined the dials to see if they could have produced the phantom light. Nothing appeared to be out of order, so Paula went ahead and developed the film. Miraculously, none of the shots she had taken were ruined.

Sheila Blackmon, who now works in the Julia Tutwiler Library at UWA, worked as a reporter for the *Meridian Star* in the late 1990s. Sheila recalled that new employees were warned against venturing into certain parts of the building alone. For Sheila, the creepiest room in the *Meridian Star* building was the break room. "I have felt things in there," Sheila said,

> *but I can't tell anymore if it's genuine or if I am thinking of those stories I have heard. I have walked through the break room and felt such a strange urge to start running that it's incredible. I've actually had to clench my fists and force myself to walk slowly in the room without looking from side to side because I have felt so frightened. Somebody better trained in the paranormal than I am could probably talk more authoritatively about the cold spots because there are places in that building that are really cold. That could just be cracks letting the cold in, but the disturbing feelings are something else altogether.*

On one Sunday in April in the 1990s, a local ghost hunting group, Orbservations, conducted a midday investigation of the *Meridian Star* offices. In an interview with staff writer Ida Brown, the director of the group, Gigi Ahrens, said that the group became interested in visiting the building after hearing stories of employees feeling fingers on the backs of their necks. People have also reported seeing strange shapes out of the corners of their eyes and hearing someone calling their names. Gigi and four other members of Orbservations walked through the building for four hours, taking digital photographs, collecting EVPs, taking temperature readings, measuring electromagnetic fields and videotaping. The most compelling piece of evidence the group collected that afternoon was a very active orb that one of members captured on video. "It was a very, very bright solid orb, and it just slowly came through the room," Gigi said. "It manifested right in front of the press—we got that on camera—and it moved slowly. I mean, really slow. It just kind of inched across the screen. And then it stopped, continued on, stopped and just kept on going."

Most of the longtime employees of the *Meridian Star* have made their peace with the old building's apparitions. Occasionally, though, the hairs still stand up on their arms when they hear strange noises or see phantoms walking through the building. Ironically, the story that has eluded the inquiring reporters of the newspaper offices for many years concerns the origins of the *Meridian's Star*'s playful spirits.

The Hotel Meridian

One of Meridian's most successful businessmen around the turn of the nineteenth century was Louis H. Arky. He owned and operated Arky's Clothing Store at the corner of Fifth Street and Twenty-second Avenue for many years. After the construction of the Union Depot in 1906, Arky realized that money could be made by catering to the passengers who were being transported to Meridian by train. At the time, Meridian's best hotel, the Great Southern, was several blocks away from the train depot. In August 1907, Arky opened a new five-story hotel—the Hotel Meridian—only two blocks away from Union Depot. He built his state-of-the-art hotel on the site of the city's first opera house, where the Mississippi Democratic Convention of 1871 was held.

Promoted as Meridian's first fireproof hotel, the Hotel Meridian was also wired for electricity. It soon became immensely popular with railroad men, who stayed in rooms furnished with electric lighting and ceiling fans after completing their runs in Meridian. The amenities offered by the Hotel Meridian also attracted traveling salesmen, who rode the trains to Meridian to sell their wares. The Hotel Meridian's appeal was also enhanced by its restaurant, which became renowned for its upscale cuisine. In 1933, the Lauderdale County Centennial Edition of the *Meridian Star* praised the Hotel Meridian for "still rendering the best of hotel service, at reasonable rates."

By this time, the hotel had been taken over by Louis Arky's son, Herbert H. Arky. After World War II, when many inner-city hotels were beginning

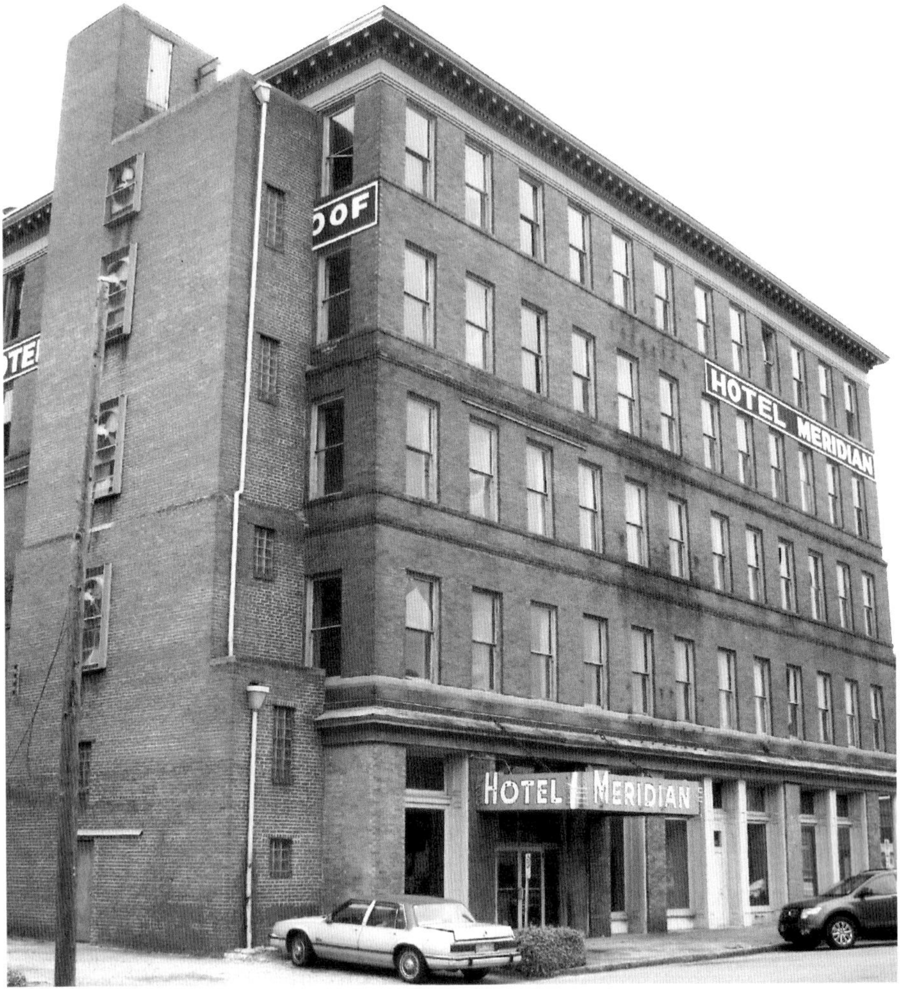

Hotel Meridian.

to lose their luster, the Hotel Meridian began to cater more and more to people desiring a permanent place of residence. People were still staying in the Hotel Meridian in the 1970s, but it was abandoned in the late 1980s.

Today, the Hotel Meridian is an empty shell, a lonely reminder of Meridian's glory days as one of the most important stops along the railroad. No one lives there now except for varmints, the occasional transient and, some say, a few ghosts. Police officers are occasionally dispatched to the

Meridian when they receive calls of suspicious activity in and around the old building. One of these officers, Steve Thomas, said that he and another officer entered the hotel one night in July 2010 when they discovered that one of the doors was standing wide open. As they carefully made their way through the darkness with their flashlights, someone—or something—threw a light bulb at them from the other end of the hallway. They searched for the person who had thrown the bulb but were unable to locate the culprit.

Thinking that the hotel might be haunted, Steve put his cellphone on voice record and proceeded to ask the spirits a number of different questions. When they returned to the station, the policemen listened to the recording they had made. They were surprised to find that they had collected three EVPs as responses to their questions. The first question Thomas asked was, "Why are you here?" The response he received was: "Where can we be?" Thomas then asked the spirit, "Did you die here?" On the recording, the officers clearly heard the word "No" after Thomas asked the question. Thomas's partner decided to antagonize the spirit, but the response on the recording was unintelligible. Former historical preservationist Fonda Rush cannot give a specific reason why the Hotel Meridian might be haunted. She thinks it is possible that someone could have died of natural causes or committed suicide in one of the rooms, both of which are common scenarios in many historic hotels.

In 2011, the fate of the Hotel Meridian is uncertain. It has been purchased by Meridian Arts and Entertainment, which could gut the hotel and transform it into an arts center or raze it entirely and start over from the ground up. If the building is remodeled or demolished, chances are good that whatever is staying there now will simply take up residence in the building that replaces it.

BRIKALO

Brikalo, which is located five miles northeast of Lauderdale in Lauderdale County, is now a private residence. However, when it was built in the 1790s by Vincent Delk, the old house served as a stagecoach stop for weary travelers making their way along the Choctaw Trail, which ran between Gainesville, Alabama, and Philadelphia, Mississippi. The original owners now rest in the Delk Family Cemetery, not far from the house. During the Civil War, General Sherman's troops attempted to burn down the stagecoach stop by throwing lighted torches onto the roof. The torches burned a hole in the roof ten feet in diameter before a bucket brigade of slaves quenched the fire and saved the house. In 1974, the house was purchased by Chatt and Harriet McGonagill. Chatt, a former executive office at the Naval Air Station, Meridian, is now retired from the U.S. Navy. His wife, Harriet, was a fifth grade teacher at Southeast Lauderdale School. Between 1974 and 1975, the McGonagill family moved in and restored the old stagecoach stop, which they named Brikalo, a name derived from the names of their children: Brian, Karen and Lori.

Despite the McGonagills' attempts to make their new home their own, including doing much of the restoration work themselves, they soon discovered that members of the previous families who had lived in the old stagecoach stop still claimed it as their own.

In an article that appeared in the October 30, 1983 edition of the *Meridian Star*, Harriet McGonagill wrote of the strange experiences they had in their first decade in the house. She said that even before she and Chatt purchased the old house, they had heard ghost stories about the old stagecoach stop from the locals. They found out that one of the ghosts was the spirit of a beautiful woman with long blond hair that cascaded around her shoulders. She has been seen many times over the years, waving from an upstairs window. Harriet also heard the legend of a five-year-old girl who fell off the stairwell near an upstairs bedroom and broke her neck while reaching through the banister for a kitten. When the McGonagills inquired about a hole in the ceiling, they were told the story about a young man who was accidentally killed with a shotgun in the front room. The hole in the ceiling was made by the blast of the shotgun. The ghosts whose identities have not been determined are probably the spirits of the patients of Dr. Silliman, some of whom succumbed to their injuries and their illnesses inside Brikalo. He practiced medicine inside the former stagecoach stop from 1869 until his death in 1904.

Harriet said that when she and her husband purchased the old house in 1974, it had stood abandoned for over twenty years. The first family members to spend a night on the property were Grandmother and Grandfather McGonagill. They were sleeping in their camper, which was parked near Brikalo, when Grandfather McGonagill happened to peer out one of the windows. He was staring at the house when he noticed a woman with long blond hair waving at him from one of the upstairs windows. He was so shaken by the apparition that he refused to spend a night inside the house.

Just before the restoration of the house began, Chatt and Harriet decided to spend a night there. They decided to sleep in the upstairs bedroom that Dr. Silliman had used as his office. Harriet crawled into her sleeping bag on the floor and was preparing to go to sleep when she noticed that a security light was shining through the window. Chatt told her that the problem would be solved when the new draperies were installed. Until then, however, Harriet would just have to put up with the inconvenience. She responded by exclaiming, "All right, but for tonight, I just wish the light was out." Suddenly, the light went out on its own. The room was immediately plunged into darkness. Harriet grabbed a flashlight and proceeded to shine it outside the window. Chatt was puzzled because the fact that the children were watching television downstairs proved that there was electricity inside the house. With an exasperated look on her face, Harriet responded, "Well, I don't care. I just wish the thing would come on." Sure enough, the light came back on.

After the McGonagills moved in, they set up an antique wind-up pendulum clock in one of the downstairs rooms. Chatt was the only member of the family who knew how to open up the clock and set it. One day, Chatt was gone on a cross-country flight. That evening, Harriet walked past the old clock and noticed that it had stopped. Harriet resigned herself to the fact that the clock could not be reset until her husband returned home, so she went to bed. The next morning, Harriet was walking past the room with the clock. She was shocked to discover that not only had someone wound the clock, but it had also been reset to the correct time. Chatt was not due to return home for several hours.

One day, Harriet and her two daughters were sitting in the room that was later converted into a kitchen. The house was not air-conditioned at the time, so the windows were open to allow the air to circulate through the house. Because the screens had not yet been installed, bugs were flying into the house. Lori, who seemed to be the bugs' favorite target, suddenly exclaimed, "I can take the heat better than the bugs!" As if in compliance with her wishes, one of the windows slammed shut. Three seconds later, another window slammed shut. Harriet said that after spending a few months in their new home, her family became very careful about what they wished for.

After awhile, the resident spirit—or spirits—seemed to have accepted the new occupants of the old stagecoach stop. Harriet and Chatt were sitting in their living room one evening when Harriet's attention was drawn through one of the windows to the porch swing, which was swinging back and forth, just as it would if someone were sitting in it. This time, Harriet felt that their ghost was comfortable sharing its house with the McGonagills.

Except for a few tense moments when the McGonagills have been startled or awakened by loud noises, they have never considered the ghosts in their house to be malevolent. Speaking of the adjustments she and her family had to make in their attitudes toward the supernatural, Harriet said, "As might be expected from a place that has existed for so long, there have been occurrences that might be considered unusual, but to our family, these incidents have been accepted as friendly gestures from our 'hosts' (not ghosts!)."

F.W. Williams House

The F.W. Williams House was originally constructed at 3128 Eighth Street. Work on the house was completed in 1886. The house had all of the amenities that any upscale Victorian family could desire, including coal-burning fireplaces, an elevator and inside bathrooms, which were added in the early 1900s. The owner, F.W. Williams, built the Victorian Queen Anne–style home as a wedding present to his wife, Mamie. Williams, who was born in 1861, was described by his friends and neighbors as a true southern gentleman. Apparently, Williams also had a keen eye for business. He founded the F.W. Williams State Agency of USF&G and was instrumental in the development of Mississippi's insurance industry. Williams also owned the Williams Funeral Home.

Shortly after Mr. and Mrs. Williams were married, her sister, Mrs. Daisy Watson, came to live with them. According to former historical preservationist Fonda Rush, Daisy was in her twenties at the time and unmarried. Apparently, she was becoming something of an embarrassment to her family in Virginia when Mamie invited her sister to come down to Mississippi and work in the insurance office. Daisy Watson soon became the first woman in Mississippi to become a partner in an insurance agency. Fearing that Daisy would never marry, Mamie eventually deeded her house to her sister. In her later years, Mamie was confined to a wheelchair. One day, Mamie was on the second floor, and she pushed the button for the elevator to come up. The door opened, and Mamie, without looking, wheeled herself through the entranceway. For some unknown reason, the elevator had not

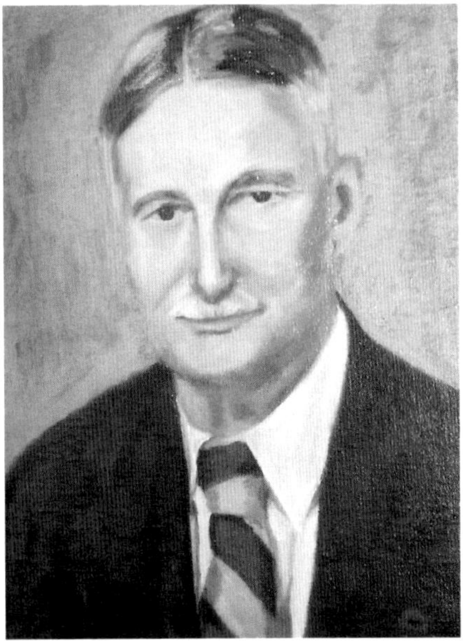

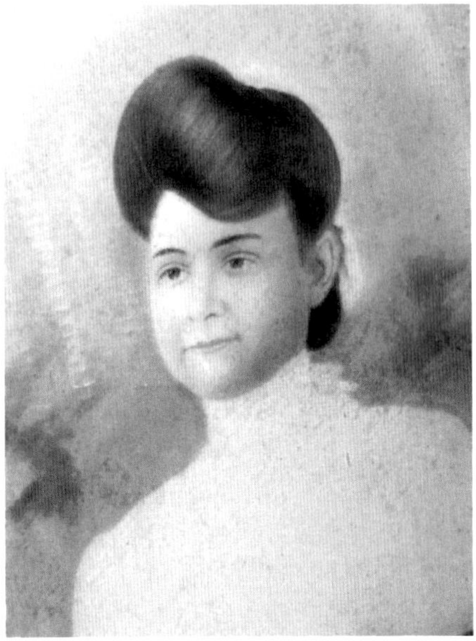

Above, left: Portrait of F.W. Williams.
Above, right: Portrait of Mrs. Mamie Williams.

Below: The F.W. Williams House.

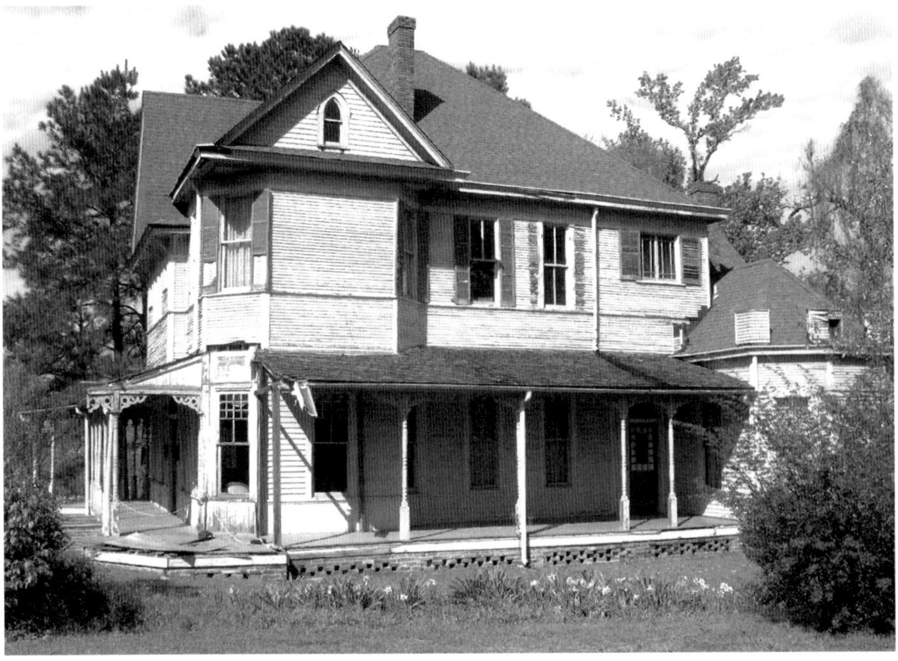

risen to the second floor, and Mamie and her wheelchair plummeted down the shaft. Despite her severe injuries, Mamie lingered for another week before finally dying. She was in her eighties at the time.

After Mamie Williams's death, Daisy Watson continued living in the house until her death at age 104 in 1978. For the sake of propriety, F.W. Williams moved out of the beautiful home he had built for his late wife. He died in 1949, not long after his wife's death. Of course, tongues began wagging in Meridian not long after Mamie's death. The coroner ignored the rumors that were flying around the city at the time and ruled Mamie's death "accidental."

In 1978, the F.W. Williams House was donated to the Meridian Restoration Foundation by granddaughter Hazel Wright, who had been married in front of the large pier mirror in the ladies' parlor. On November 18, 1979, the old house was moved to its present location at 905 Martin Luther King Drive. Today, the F.W. Williams House stands as a monument to one of the city's most prominent families.

Because a violent death took place inside the F.W. Williams House, many residents of Meridian have naturally assumed that it must be haunted. In 2004, along with disc jockeys Scotty Ray Boyd and Debbie Alexander and several guests, I tested the validity of these rumors by spending the night inside the old mansion. I walked through the house with my EMF detector, my tape recorder and my digital camera in an attempt to capture EVPs

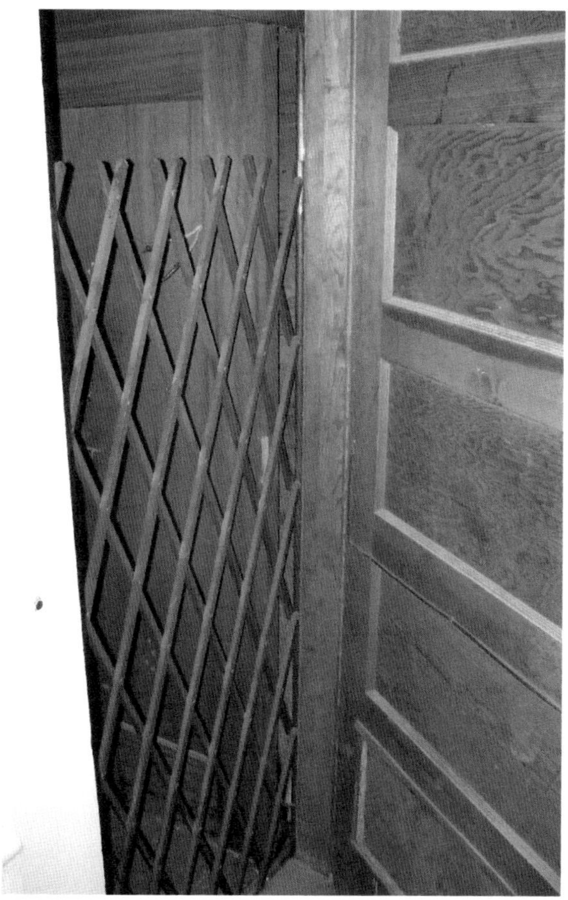

Mrs. Mamie Williams rolled her wheelchair through the door of this elevator and plunged to her death.

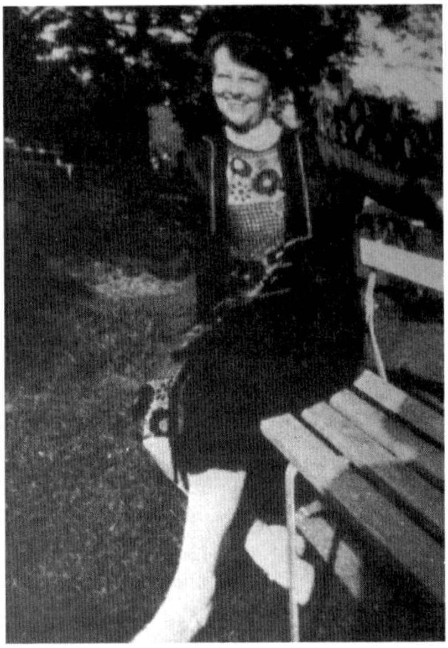

Daisy Watson.

and, hopefully, an orb. That night, I slept on the floor in Mr. Williams's bedroom, across from the fatal elevator. During the night, my sleep was disturbed—not by paranormal activity, but by the pain that shot through my back from sleeping on a hard, wooden floor. The next morning, I spoke with the other members of the group and discovered that no one had any ghostly encounters. After returning home, I examined the photographs I had taken and the tape I had recorded. I discovered that I did not have a shred of evidence of the paranormal.

Our inability to collect any hard proof of the existence of the paranormal during our one-night investigation does not mean that the F.W. Williams House is not haunted. Chances are that we might have actually collected some genuine evidence had we returned to the F.W. Williams House. In fact, a different ghost-hunting group claimed to have collected a number of EVPs and orbs during its investigation in 2009. However, if the people who work in the Office Plaza on the former location of the F.W. Williams House can be believed, the ghost of Mamie Williams remained at the house's original location on Eighth Street.

In 2000, Fonda Rush received a strange phone call from the Mississippi Department of Health. "They said that their offices are haunted, and they believe that [their haunting] had a connection to the Williams House. So they came and had their Christmas party at the F.W. Williams House." Apparently, the people who worked in the Office Plaza soon after its construction reported hearing knocking sounds and footsteps. Sometimes, objects that were placed in one specific spot were found in an entirely different room the next morning. Fonda agrees that the spirit of one of the original occupants of the F.W. Williams House has a very strong attachment to Eighth Street. "Maybe if there is a ghost," she says, "it went right back to where the house was originally."

CAMP BINACHI

Frank Polizzi, who has worked as a volunteer at Camp Binachi since 1985, is Meridian's resident expert on the Boy Scout camp. "I think the camp has been around since the early 1930s," Frank said. "It was donated by the Brookshire family." Frank is also a fine storyteller, whose version of Lauderdale County's best-known campfire story—the tale of a headless Indian chief—has been terrifying Boy Scouts for decades. The following is Frank Pilozzi's account of the legend of "Old Moss Back":

The story is the legend of Camp Binachi. I really don't know its origin. I've been telling this story since the middle 1980s. I am a Scout leader. Actually, at this point in time, I train other Scout leaders. I don't have a single unit, like I used to. I heard the story from older Scout leaders. Scouting is based a lot on Indian lore. They didn't have a written language, so all of their stories were passed down orally. So this story fits in really well with scouting. It adds to the ambience of the camping experience. It has really been carried on at Camp Binachi. Whoever I talk to, be it a former Scout or a brand-new one, they remember the story. I wasn't raised in this area. I came here as a young adult. I hear other people talk about Moss Back.

We have a small amphitheater on the other side of the lake where we tell the story. It has a beautiful view of the lake. I never did get the names or the particulars. I assume it was the Choctaw Indians. The story is about a tribe of Indians who lived around Lake Williams, which is the center of Camp Binachi. Tradition dictated that whoever the brave was who moved

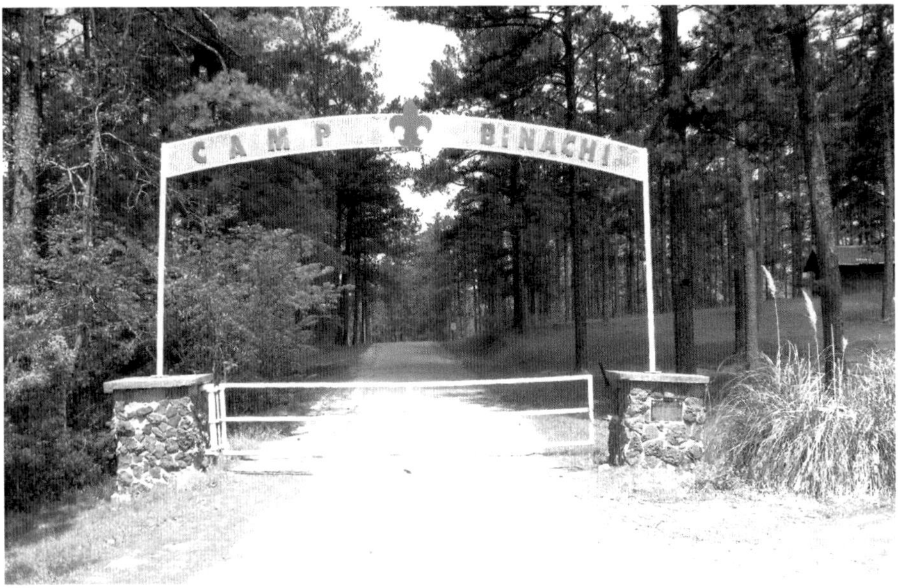

Entrance to Camp Binachi.

up to the position of Indian chief, he remained the chief until his death, whether that death be by natural causes or whether he lost his life in battle. Or the final option was a younger brave who wanted to be chief challenged the older chief in a battle to the death. The story goes that a young brave decided that it was time for him to become chief.

The old chief knew that he was getting older, and the young brave knew it was time for a change. One day, the old chief stepped out of his teepee, and there stood the young brave in a challenging position, with his legs spread, staring down the chief. The chief knew that meant that it was time for him to fight for his right to remain chief. The chief walked up to him, and they engaged in a battle. They fought up and down and back and forth. I point out that the fight occurred up in these hills somewhere. They fought all morning and into the afternoon. They fought so hard that the earth trembled and the trees shook. The fight continued up through the late afternoon and into the darkness.

This is a typical campfire story, so we tell it at night. We pause at times to point out that it was a night like tonight. If there is a moon out, we say there was a bright moon that night. If not, we say there were stars in the sky. We try to get the audience involved. We want them to feel that they were there during the actual battle.

They fought back and forth until they could hardly stand up. At this point, Moss Back, as old as he was, managed to push the brave down. I wave my arms to show how the brave fell backwards and hit the ground. The young brave knew by this time that it was over, that he would not become the chief of the tribe. Moss Back lunged toward him, and the brave was trying to scurry away from the older Indian when he felt something in his right hand. It was his tomahawk. The young brave, with his last ounce of strength, stood up, and with one mighty blow, he swung his tomahawk and cut off Moss Back's head. His head rolled down one of these hills and into this lake. I pause for effect sometimes. Then I tell them that Moss Back stood up and ran off into the woods without his head. The legend goes that at night, Moss Back still goes around the lake, searching for his head.

There are a few things that would discourage Moss Back from coming around people. He doesn't like a lot of noise, so we tell them that when they are with a group of people and they see him, they should yell, "Run! Run! Run!" Then I play a game with them. I tell them to yell "Run! Run! Run!" if I mention the name "Moss Back" again. So while we are sitting

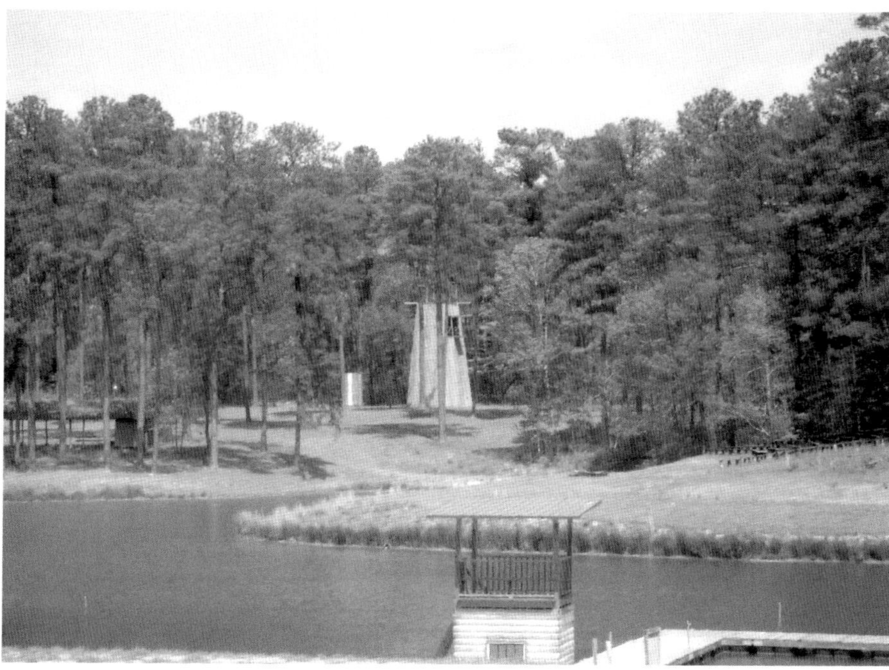

According to legend, the decapitated head of a Choctaw Indian chief rolled into this lake.

around the campfire talking, we will inject Moss Back somewhere into the conversation—"Has anyone seen Moss Back?" Then someone will yell, "Run! Run! Run!" and I say, "You'd better be a little louder than that." They enjoy that, at least most of them do. Some of them get a bit concerned.

The other protection can be found on the other side of the dining hall. If you are facing the dining hall from the road, there is a forked road that leads into a small camp called Trail's Peak. There's a tall stone that sticks up from a concrete slab. It's a concrete column called the Moss Back Stone. According to the legend, if you rub that stone after dark, Moss Back will not harm you during the night. So, naturally, after the campfire breaks up, we have around a hundred Cub Scouts trying to find their way to the Moss Back Stone. It's a combination of a legend and some fun and games for the Scouts. It's been carried on for years and years since the late 1920s and early 1930s. That's basically the story. I'm sure each version of it has a different twist to it. I get a little more theatrical when I tell the story in front of a group of people. I've been called on many times by many groups to tell this story, whether it's the younger Cub Scouts or the older Boy Scouts. I guess I have been telling this story longer than anybody.

THE OLE STENNIS PLACE

The Ole Stennis Place was built at 7812 King's Road in 1857 by Hays Rodgers, who was born in Greene County, Tennessee, on February 1, 1793. Hays had fought in the War of 1812 in Major Dale's Battalion, Mississippi Militia, and in the Fifteenth Regiment, Mississippi Militia. Hays married his wife, the former Mary A. Scott, on December 16, 1816. The Rodgerses' home is not only the first house in Lauderdale County that was not constructed of logs, but it is also the oldest house in the county.

Hays Rodgers died in December 1862, and his house was sold to Major Adam T. Stennis on the steps of the Lauderdale County Courthouse in 1869. Adam Stennis was the great-uncle of U.S. senator John C. Stennis. The purchase price also included a carriage house, a barn and stable and a smokehouse. Members of the Stennis family continued living in the old house until the late 1970s. The house stood vacant during the 1980s and the early 1990s.

When Jeannie and William Hover moved into the Ole Stennis Place in 2002, the old house was so covered with vines that it was barely visible from the road. When the Hovers examined the house closely, they were surprised that it was in pretty good shape, with the exception of the front porch, most of which had to be replaced. They decided to preserve the historical integrity of the historic house as much as possible. Consequently, the doors, walls, blown-glass windows, pine floors and inlaid brick walkway out front look much the same as they did in the 1850s. Hooks that once held lanterns are still firmly anchored in the kitchen ceiling. The Hovers even found the

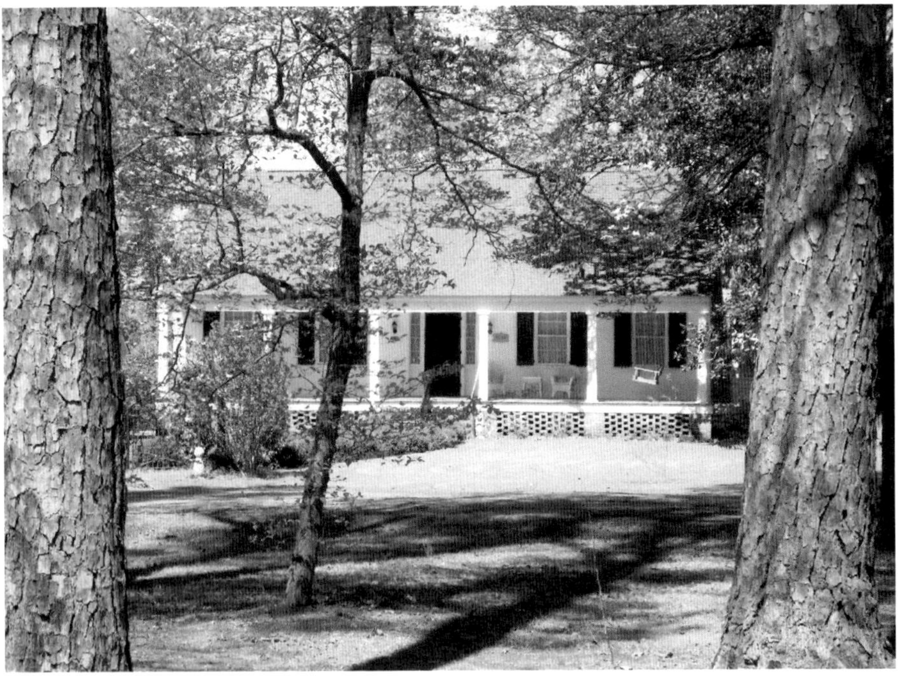

The Ole Stennis Place.

keys to the original locks. By the time Jeannie and Bill moved in, the barn, stable, smokehouse and carriage house were gone, and only two hundred acres were still on the property lines.

Jeannie Hover's beautiful old home could be haunted by the ghosts of one of Hays and Mary's fourteen children. "We hear voices from time to time," Jeannie said. "My daughter has sworn she hears children running through the house. One night, my daughter and some of her friends were having a sleepover in the house when they heard children running up and down the hallway. They were so scared that they left the house at 2:00 a.m." On a different occasion, Jeannie was working inside the house when she heard her husband call her name. She searched the entire house for him but could not find him. It turned out that she was alone in the house at the time. "A few days later, the same thing happened to Bill," Jeannie said. "He was inside the house when he heard my voice call his name. I wasn't there, and no one else was either."

Another owner said he saw the porch swing start swinging on its own while at the same time the piano started playing on its own. The mischievous antics of the Rodgers children seem to have enhanced the homey atmosphere of the Ole Stennis Place, despite the fact that they have been dead for many years.

Miraculously, the Ole Stennis Place has survived the ravages of time and neglect for over 150 years. Ironically, when Hurricane Katrina raged through Lauderdale County in 2005, the Ole Stennis Place was one of the only homes in the Pines Springs Community that still had electricity. For a while, Jeannie and Bill operated the Ole Stennis Place as a bed-and-breakfast. In December 2006, Jeannie had an open house to benefit Love's Kitchen, which was still under construction at the time. Visitors paid five dollars or offered canned goods to catch a glimpse of frontier life in Lauderdale County. Many of the visitors—myself included—were not at all surprised to discover that some of the history of the old house appears to have stuck around in a less tangible form.

LAUDERDALE COUNTY COURTHOUSE

Lauderdale County was established in 1833, three years after the signing of the Treaty of Dancing Rabbit. The little community of Marion, which was named after the "Swamp Fox," Francis Marion, was originally named as the county seat. Then, in 1870, the county seat was moved a few miles southwest of Marion to Meridian as the result of a public referendum. Lauderdale County's first courthouse was built in 1890. However, it burned down in 1903, and a new courthouse was erected on the same site between 1904 and 1905. Constructed in the Beaux Arts style, the courthouse sported a dome with cupola, as well as a number of sculpted figures, which were removed sometime around World War I. A Confederate memorial was constructed on the northwest corner of the site.

Several major structural changes were made in 1939 as part of the Federal Works Project. Not only was the entire building enlarged and remodeled in the Art Deco style, but a jail was built on the top floor of the building as well. According to Ward Calhoun Sr., director of the Lauderdale Department of Archives and History, for years people have said that when the courthouse dome was removed, it was put away in storage, but no one knows where it is.

Rumors of the ghosts haunting the Lauderdale County Courthouse have been floating around Meridian for many years. However, the first published account of haunted activity inside the old building appeared in the October 27, 1980 edition of the *Meridian Star*. According to staff writer Sidney Cearnal, items filed away in the cabinets in the circuit clerk's office

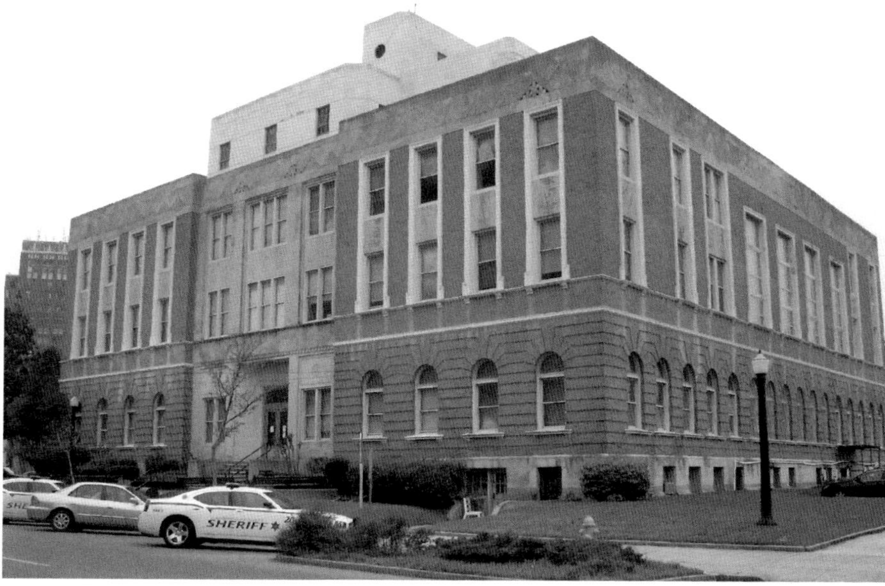

The Lauderdale County Courthouse.

mysteriously disappeared, only to return a few days later. District 5 election commissioner Lorita Mitcham said, "My list of poll workers disappeared just before the September 5 deadline, but it was back last week." She added that a copy of the payroll for a previous special election also disappeared. It turned up later in another commissioner's drawer. Barbara Henson, who was District 3 commissioner at the time, said that she had heard about the lists of poll workers vanishing, but she was unaffected by whoever—or whatever—was responsible.

In 1983, a paralegal named Holly and her boss stayed after-hours in the courthouse to look up some information in the archives for a case they were working on. After a few minutes, they heard the sound of doors opening and closing in the hallway. The pair ignored the sounds and continued working. After awhile, Holly's boss left her alone in the archives to go get some coffee. He had not been gone for very long before Holly heard a door close in the hallway. She stuck her head out the door and looked up and down the hallway, but no one was there. Holly was beginning to feel uneasy, so she proceeded to walk down the hallway in search of the lawyer. Suddenly, she heard another door open and close. Thinking that her boss was "messing with her," Holly returned to the archives. Just as she started to sit down, Holly heard another door open and close. Holly's curiosity temporarily overcame the sense of dread that was beginning to creep over her, so she went back out into the hallway and jiggled the doorknobs to the offices. They were all locked. At this point, Holly realized that something highly unusual was happening. She was walking back to the archives when she heard footsteps behind her. Holly spun around, but no one was there. She rushed back to the archives, threw herself into the chair and began writing furiously. Holly breathed a huge sigh of relief when her boss appeared in the doorway

The courthouse ghost continued to be an active presence in the 2000s. Julia Marshall, who works in the tax assessor's office, says that the ghost has been given a name: Boots. "I have heard him in the front part of the office at night or when I am alone in the office," Julia said. "I have heard noises, not footsteps. There have been times when Boots has gotten the best of me, and I had to leave."

A maintenance worker named Rhonda has had a number of terrifying experiences in the courthouse. "One time, I was vacuuming in the courtroom on the third floor," Rhonda said. "I was cleaning up when I heard the elevator bell. The door to the elevator opened up, but there was nobody there. I kept on working, and I heard a door creak open. Then I heard somebody talking. I looked around the courtroom, but I didn't see anyone. I said to myself, 'It's time to go,' and I left."

Rhonda had an even closer encounter with the paranormal a few weeks later when she was working in the courtroom on the second floor. "I was vacuuming when I heard a roaring noise," Rhonda said.

> *Then the lights went out, and then they came back on. I walked over to the jury room and started cleaning. When I came out of the jury room, I saw a blond lady in a white dress sitting in one of the chairs. I got out of there so fast. I left my cleaning cart and didn't go back for it until somebody could come with me. This happened on the weekend when nobody else was there.*

Rhonda says that the jury room on the second floor is weird for another reason. "In the jury box, I sometimes find a film on the back of the chairs," Rhonda said. "I'll clean it up and go back a couple of days later, and the film will be back on the chairs. I don't know what it is."

Rhonda has had so many unexplainable encounters in the courthouse that she is, admittedly, a bit jumpy at times. "If someone comes up behind me and doesn't call my name, they're going to get sprayed with whatever I got in my hand," she said.

A secretary named Valarie also got a little closer to Boots than she would have liked. One day, she walked into one of the courtrooms to get something off the judge's desk. In this particular courtroom, the door locked from the outside with a key and from the inside with a deadlock. When she walked over to the door to leave, she noticed that it had been deadlocked from the inside. At that terrifying moment, Valarie realized that someone—or something—was in the courtroom with her. She opened the door and left in a hurry.

Several years ago, a city policeman was preparing to leave the building at 3:00 a.m. When he walked through the third-floor library, a book flew off the shelf and came right at him. The policeman locked up the building and walked over to his car, which was parked on the west side of the building. He started to pull out when he looked back at the courthouse and noticed that all of the lights were on. He was certain that he had turned off all the lights before he left.

Strange incidents have occurred so often at the courthouse that, for some employees, they have become commonplace. Some employees hear doors slamming late at night when they are the only ones inside the building. Others have claimed to feel someone standing behind them when they walk into the elevator. Some employees are so afraid of running into the ghost that they are reluctant to enter the building at night. Granted, not everyone who works at the Lauderdale County Courthouse has had a paranormal experience, but the people who have seen or heard Boots are likely to keep the ghost stories alive for some time to come.

Peavey Melody Music

On March 2, 1906, Meridian experienced the worst natural disaster in its recorded history. At 6:30 p.m., a massive tornado ravaged the Queen City. Described by the *Meridian Golden Age* as a "black funnel cloud of death," the tornado blew in from the southwest with no warning. The first building hit by the tornado was the Meridian Fertilizer Factory. The Meridian Planing Mill and the Meridian Light and Railway Plant, at Twenty-seventh Avenue, were the next buildings to be leveled. The tornado then swerved to the east and destroyed the New Orleans and Northeastern freight company. By the time the funnel cloud had moved on to Bonita, it had demolished almost every building between Twenty-second and Twenty-fourth Avenues, including two to three blocks of stores, five city churches and a number of private residences. Twenty-three people died, and thirty people were severely injured. Seventeen people who sought refuge in the dining room of the Elmore Hotel were killed when the building collapsed. Two people perished in the fires that swept through the ruins. More lives would probably have been lost, especially along Front Street, had the tornado struck Meridian in the morning or afternoon.

One of the city's newspapers described the devastation wrought by the tornado as "three miles of debris, three miles of despair." Within a few days, martial law was declared in Meridian. The entire perimeter of the disaster zone, starting along Front Street and stretching from Twenty-sixth to Nineteenth Street, was patrolled by soldiers. Convicts from the Rankin County penal facility were brought to Meridian to assist with the cleanup.

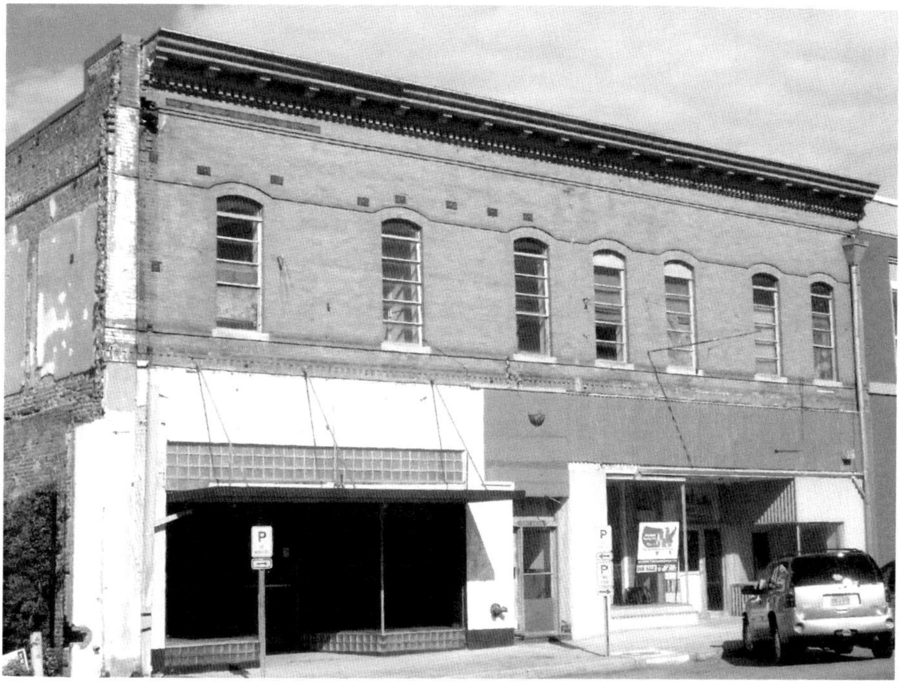

Peavey Melody Music is housed in a former funeral home.

A train carrying Governor James K. Vardaman, Attorney General Williams and forty senators arrived at what was left of the depot to inspect the damage. Miraculously, many of the businesses and industries that had been reduced to rubble eventually recovered, and Merdian's population resumed its rapid growth. Today, the suffering inflicted on the citizens of Meridian by nature's fury is a fading memory, kept alive in history books, the local archives and one of the city's most fascinating ghost stories.

Many of the casualties were taken to the Smith Funeral Parlor, located in the Wagoner Annex No. 3. The victims, most of whom were children, were carried through the first floor and up to a large room on the second floor, where they were stacked up like cordwood. Injured people were placed next to the corpses. During the course of the night, a number of them succumbed to their injuries inside the funeral parlor before medical assistance arrived. According to legend, the injuries suffered by the dead and dying were so severe that the path the rescuers took as they carried them across the first floor was stained with blood. The blood resisted all attempts to have it removed, so the owner of the building covered the bloody trail with tile.

The history of the Wagoner Annex No. 3 entered a second phase in 1938, when Joseph B. "Mutt" Peavey opened Peavey Melody Music in the old building on Twenty-second Avenue. The next year, Mutt penned the Mississippi State University fight song, "Hail State." In 1952, up-and-coming rock-'n'-roller Elvis Presley, who was competing in the Jimmie Rodgers Festival at the time, visited the store. In 1955, Mutt's fourteen-year-old son, Hartley Peavey, created his first amplifier from a television power transformer and other spare parts. After graduating from Mississippi State University, Hartley opened his amplifier business inside his parents' basement, but when demand for his amplifiers increased, he moved his operation out of the home to the second floor of Peavey Melody Music in 1966. Two years later, Hartley's business had grown so much that he moved out of his father's store and into another building. Today, Peavey's is one of Meridian's largest employers. In fact, Peavey's products have had such an impact on the music scene that for years, visitors from all over the world visited Peavey's Melody Music just to catch a glimpse of where it all started.

No one knows for sure when the ghostly activity in the music store actually began. Berry Grey, who began working at Peavey's Melody Music in 1969 and bought the business in 1987, had his first encounter in the late 1970s. He and a co-worker were working in the store one Saturday in the dead of winter. The two men usually took turns locking up on Saturdays, so about thirty minutes before closing time, Berry told his friend to go home. After his co-worker left, Berry was in the process of straightening up the store when he heard the sound of children running and laughing on the second floor. Children had been in and out of the store all day, taking piano and guitar lessons upstairs, so Berry assumed that several of the children were still upstairs.

> *I went back to the doorway under the balcony, and I poked my head up the stairway and yelled, "Be careful of that elevator shaft." I was thinking, "Oh, Jesus. Somebody must have left that door to the long hallway open. The piano teacher's not looking after those kids." All I heard was laughing and running. I walked upstairs and found the lights were off, so I clicked them on and said, "You guys are supposed to be downstairs." I didn't see anybody, but I continued to hear giggling, and it was starting to get colder. When I heard someone moving around one of the rooms, I turned around and said* [to myself], *"Feet, don't fail me now!" I went straight out the door, down the stairs and locked the store up.*

Another employee who has had a brush with the paranormal inside Peavey Melody Music is Robert Holcomb. In 1995, he said, "We heard noises upstairs, and Mr. Grey said, 'Who's that upstairs?' We could hear the sound of little feet walking back and forth." On August 30, 2005, Robert's family experienced the bizarre occurrences at Peavey Melody Music:

> *The day after Katrina hit Meridian,* [my wife] *Melanie and* [my son] *Sam and I decided to spend the night at the music store because it had electricity and our home didn't. Sam slept upstairs, and Melanie and I slept in the studio downstairs. In the middle of the night, Sam asked us who turned the music on. Sure enough, a Chuck Mangione song was blasting through the store's sound system. I have no idea who turned it on.*

Virginia Raymond, who worked for Peavey's Melody Music for more than five decades, probably had the greatest knowledge of the store's paranormal activity, simply because she worked there for so long. She frequently cautioned people against climbing the stairs to the second floor. "You'all be careful," she'd say, "'cause they're up there."

Peavey Melody Music closed in 2007 after the death of owner Berry Grey. Today, the historic building stands vacant. The tiled walkway cutting through the faded carpeting on the first floor is the only tangible reminder of that dark March day in 1906 when Meridian first felt the brunt of nature's wrath.

THE HAUNTED BARN

For centuries, the bond between man and dog has been imbued with sentimentality and romanticism. It is no small wonder, then, that a dog's undying love for its owner has become the stuff of folklore. In fact, ghost dogs have become a staple of southern ghost stories. A good example is the "long, low dog" of Sevierville, Tennessee. The dog was killed by the infamous "land pirate" John Murriell, and its ghost is still seen loping along a lonely road outside Surgoinsville, Tennessee. In Meridian, one can also find a tale of a dog that refused to allow death to separate it from its owner.

Faye Gullette taught reading at Northwest Middle School until her retirement in 2008. For years, Faye lived in an apartment above a barn about six miles northeast of Meridian. "We had a lot of animals that have died that are buried around the barn," Faye said.

> *At 5:00 a.m. one morning, I was on the landing on the stairs leading down from my apartment. I had three dog houses that backed up to the barn. On that particular morning, I saw a little white shape leaving the barn. My first thought was, "That's my little dog Scruffy come over here to see me." I could see the dog houses from where I stood. The shape walked past the dog houses, and it was then that I realized that it wasn't Scruffy. It was too small. The owner of the barn came by, and I said, "Linda, I think I've seen my first ghost."*

Faye is convinced that she saw something very strange that night:

> *It was squarish. It went past me and walked right through the fence to the woods. It was thin, not solid. It didn't have any legs. It was more like a piece of gauze about the size of a flag. It made a straight line to the woods, and that's when I realized it wasn't Scruffy. It was white, and it floated about six inches above the ground. I didn't get to watch it for very long. The ghost walked in a straight line, but it bobbed up and down. When I realized it wasn't my dog, I stopped walking and really started paying attention to it. When I got to the bottom of the stairs, I realized it had gotten to the fence. I looked back, and I was like, "What is that?" I could see my dog Scruffy in the doghouse. What I saw was not the perfect shape of an animal. It just glided across the yard. I thought it was a dog until I realized it wasn't coming toward me. It passed through the rail fence. It didn't go through an opening. It never stopped. It was not in any shape or form alarming to me at all. It was almost like I was honored to catch a glimpse of it.*

As soon as Faye realized that the animal she saw was not real, she decided that it must have been the spirit of a dog that died on the property:

> *We used to have a dog out there that loved me. We got her from the dump. Every night before I'd leave the barn, I could tell she wanted to go with me. It was a beautiful little Shelty-looking dog. She adored me. One day, I didn't go back to the barn. The other dogs attacked it that night and killed it. It crawled under my trailer and died. This happened a couple of years ago. It devastated me because at night, I could tell she wanted to go home with me. She'd come with me and go to the car and try to put her little feet up there. She begged me to take her home. Looking back now, I realize that she was afraid because the other dogs were mean to her. Her name was Riblet.*

Faye Gullette is one of those animal lovers whose love for their pets borders on the maternal. She describes her relationship with her dogs as "therapeutic," suggesting that she receives more from them than she gives. She clearly felt grateful that Riblet returned from the dead just to see her one last time.

The Tinney House

Sheila Hutcherson is a nurse and aspiring writer. During the annual conference of the Mississippi Writers' Guild in Vicksburg on August 6–7, 2010, she told me about an old house in Lauderdale County, where she lived between 1992 and 1994. The house is located on Azalea Road at the intersection of what used to be Cotton Gin Road. The house, which sits on top of a hill about two hundred feet off the road, was built between 1902 and 1903 by Reba and Press Tinney. The two years when Sheila lived in the house gave her some of the most terrifying moments of her entire life.

Most of what Sheila knows about Mr. and Mrs. Tinney came from a lady in her church, Ms. Alma Phillips. "When I was living in that house, she would stop by and visit," Sheila said.

> *She told me how much Ms. Reba loved her house. Her husband died first, and she lived there until she died. I don't know if they had any children or not. Ms. Phillips said that another couple moved in after the Tinneys died. As far as Ms. Phillips knew, this couple did not have any strange experiences while living in the house. A few months later, they rented it out.*

Sheila suspected that the house might be haunted when the man she rented it from refused to go inside while she was signing the lease. "He stayed out in the yard and typed the lease on the back of his truck," Sheila said.

> *My roommate and I paid a month in advance, plus the final month's rent and a security deposit. I had graduated nursing school in 1992 and was*

living in Russell. My friend and I had been looking for a place to rent, and this was the first place we found that had land with it. Our rent was $375 a month. This was quite a chunk of change to come up with because I was still paying for nursing school, and I hadn't even started working yet.

Before Sheila and her roommate, Carla, entered the Tinney House, their landlord told them that the previous renters had left the door unlocked when they moved out, as well as leaving behind all of their possessions. "That should have been an indication that something was going on," Sheila said. However, the house suited her and her roommate's needs, so they moved in during the fall of 1992.

The first thing Sheila and her roommate noticed was that the old house had not been remodeled for years. The wooden floors in the hallway and bedrooms and the linoleum floor in the kitchen were all original. The house also had old-fashioned gas heaters, a fireplace and a single bathroom. The women immediately decided that they had to make at least a few modern improvements in the old house before they moved from their house in Russell. However, they had no sooner made a few changes than the resident ghost began making its presence known. "We were laying down some carpet remnants when I started smelling a strange perfume that I didn't recognize," Sheila said.

It smelled like a floral scent. Neither of us had washed our hair that day, so it wasn't shampoo that we were smelling. I followed the scent all over the room. Suddenly, my roommate broke the uncomfortable silence in the room. "I think there's something I need to tell you. I think we have a ghost, and I think it's a woman." A few seconds later, a window dropped in the kitchen with a loud slam. I didn't respond to what she had said. I just walked into the big old country kitchen and shut the window. All I told her was, "We're going to have to prop up the window." At this point, I didn't believe that we had a ghost.

That night, Sheila and her roommate were preparing to leave the Tinney House and return to their house in Russell. They had just climbed in the car and were about to drive away when Sheila noticed that the bathroom light was off.

I told my roommate that I thought she had turned the bathroom light on. She said that she had. I replied, "Well, it's not on now." I unlocked the

> *house and went back in and flipped the light back on. I will admit that I was beginning to feel a little creeped out. I left the house and got back in the car. We could see that the light was still on. But when we came back the next day, the bathroom light was turned off.*

For the next two weeks, after the pair moved in, someone—or something—turned the bathroom light off after they turned it on.

Soon after Sheila and Carla moved into the Tinney House, these bizarre occurrences became so commonplace that they started to seem ordinary. Sheila was jolted out of her complacency one evening while she was washing dishes. Carla had just gone to bed, and Sheila thought she was all alone in the house:

> *I was washing dishes, and I had this impulse to look behind me. I had this feeling that there was somebody standing behind me. Suddenly, it was like somebody had put his hand on my hip. I turned the water off and hollered. I ran into the bedroom and started yelling at Carla: "Get up! We've got to move! I can't stand this anymore!" Carla calmed me down after awhile. That was the only time I felt somebody touch me in that house. This happened three weeks after we first moved in.*

The paranormal activity inside the Tinney House seemed to increase over the next few months. Sheila had another ghostly experience in the Tinney House one day when she was lying on the floor with her legs propped up on the couch in an effort to relieve the stress in her back. She was totally relaxed and almost asleep when she detected the same perfume scent that she had smelled the first day she and her roommate had walked through the house. Sensing that the ghost did not want her there, Sheila spoke to it directly:

> *I don't know who you are, but we really like this house, and we don't mean you any harm. We really like this house, but you're scaring me, and I'd appreciate it if you would not make any funny noises anymore because I don't do well with ghosts.*

Sheila and Carla had only lived in the Tinney House for a few weeks when they decided that they could not share their house with a ghost. However, the women could not just pack up and leave because they had signed a year-long lease. In desperation, Sheila called the landlord and asked him if he knew the house was haunted.

He said it wasn't haunted when he was there. In fact, he acted like he was totally shocked. I was thinking, "You didn't go into that house when we were there." He just drew up the lease and handed us the keys. He denied that the house was haunted, but he had to know it was because of all these problems he had with people leaving in the middle of the night.

During Sheila and Carla's first winter in the Tinney House, they had a frightening encounter with their ghost one cold morning when they were in the bathroom.

We were just talking when we heard somebody walking around the house. Carla was already dressed so she walked out of the bathroom to see who was in the house. Carla came back in the bathroom and said, "There's somebody standing on our front porch!" By then, I had changed into clothes to feed the animals in. I walked out to the front porch, but I didn't see anybody. Because the house is on a hill, it would be hard for somebody to get off the porch in a hurry and disappear. Both of us walked down the hill, but we couldn't find anybody. When we got back to the house, Carla said all she could see was the outline of a man. She said he looked a lot like Darth Vader. He almost looked like a hooded figure. While she was watching him from the window, the apparition walked across the porch.

Most of the people who spent any time at all in the hosue left with a new attitude toward the paranormal. After Sheila and Carla were done furnishing their house, they invited two friends of theirs, Jimmy and Pat, over for dinner. "He [Jimmy] definitely did not believe in ghosts," Sheila said.

He had an explanation for everything. We were sitting around talking. We were talking about the ghost, and we heard the doorknob of the front door open. Then the front door just swung open. We all stopped and kind of looked at it for a few seconds. Then Jimmy said, "That's the wind." Immediately, the door closed. I asked Jimmy, "Is that the wind?" All he said was, "I gotta go! I gotta get up early and go to work!" And he left.

Sheila's mischievous spirit also moved objects around, usually at the most inopportune times.

One day, my friend Doug and I were building a horse barn. I had bought an expensive mare, and the little lean-to I had built wouldn't do. We had put the four-by-fours in the ground. We were using a shovel to pack down the ground around the four-by-fours. We turned the shovel upside down and laid it against the concrete. When I turned around to grab the shovel, it was gone. It was right by a big pine tree. After we got the four-by-fours in place, we were ready to start framing it up. We had nailed the two-by-fours to the four-by-fours. I laid our hammer down. It was broad daylight, and only Doug and I were there. I reached for the hammer, and it was gone. We never found it. Well, we got another hammer. When we finally got the shed to the point where we were ready to nail, we couldn't find the big keg of nails that I had put in another little shed. When I went to get the nails, they were gone, and they never turned up. I don't think anyone stole the shovel, hammer and nails because nothing else was stolen. The curious thing is, though, that when we were digging the holes with the post hole digger to put the posts in, we ran into old foundation material—rocks and stuff—and Doug said, 'We're digging through a previous building." He felt like something had already been there, so it could be that the spirits connected with this old building didn't want something else built there.

Sheila is convinced that the ghost haunting the interior of the Tinney House was the spirit of Mrs. Tinney because of a conversation she had with a nurse who worked at Rush Hospital.

I told her that I was living in a house owned by Reba Tinney, and she said, "Ms. Reba? I took care of Reba Tinney when she was a patient up here!" I asked her, "Was she one of those little old ladies who liked to wear old-fashioned perfume?" She replied, "Oh, my gosh! She had to have her perfumes and lotions!" I asked the nurse what Ms. Reba wore, and she said, "Oh, it was one of those old-fashioned perfumes, like lavender." I am sure that lavender is the scent I smelled when Carla and I first walked through the house.

Sheila moved out of the Tinney House in 1994 after living there for almost two years. Carla stayed on for a while after Sheila left. One night, she was sleeping in her bedroom when she heard a woman weeping. Carla walked out to the front porch, where she thought the sounds were coming from, but there was nobody there. Thinking that she had imagined the crying, Carla turned off the light and went back to bed. A few minutes later, she heard the weeping again. She turned on the light, but she still could not find anyone on the porch. Sheila is convinced that the weeping woman was the ghost of

Ms. Reba. "Ms. Reba loved her front porch," Sheila said. "She loved to sit on her front porch and swing. She might be angry because the new owner closed in the porch."

Almost two decades have passed since Sheila Hutcherson lived in the Tinney House. Even though the passing of time has not diminished the terror Sheila experienced, her curiosity regarding the paranormal activity remains strong. "I'd love to go back to that house again," Sheila said. "I'd love to know who owns it now. I'd like to see if I could make Ms. Reba come back."

Queen City Nursing Home

Surprisingly, nursing homes are not at the top of most paranormal investigators' lists of haunted places. After all, death is a very common occurrence in these places.

Meridian has a nursing home that has acquired a haunted reputation, but apparently not because of any deaths that occurred in that particular building. The Queen City Nursing Home is built on the site of the old two-story St. Joseph's Hospital at 1201 Eighty-ninth Avenue. Former historical preservationist Fonda Rush recalls visiting an aunt who was treated there several times in the early 1960s. Like most Catholic hospitals, St. Joseph's was staffed by nuns who served as nurses. St. Joseph's ceased operations in the 1960s after Alliance Hospital was built on Highway 39 and was eventually torn down. Fonda Rush believes that if the Queen City Nursing Home is truly haunted, it is because of its location.

In 1997, a nontraditional student at the University of West Alabama named Crystal Turner told me about one particular room that was reported to be haunted while she was working there:

> *This took place in Mr. Holland's room. He only stayed there a little while… Mr. Holland talked all the time about a little boy* [in the room]. *I had heard about the child before talking to him. When a patient is deathbed delirious and is yelling, "Get him out! Get him out!" we know that the little boy has been there. This is what happened to Mr. Holland. He was a new patient here. He had only been here a while. One day, he started calling to*

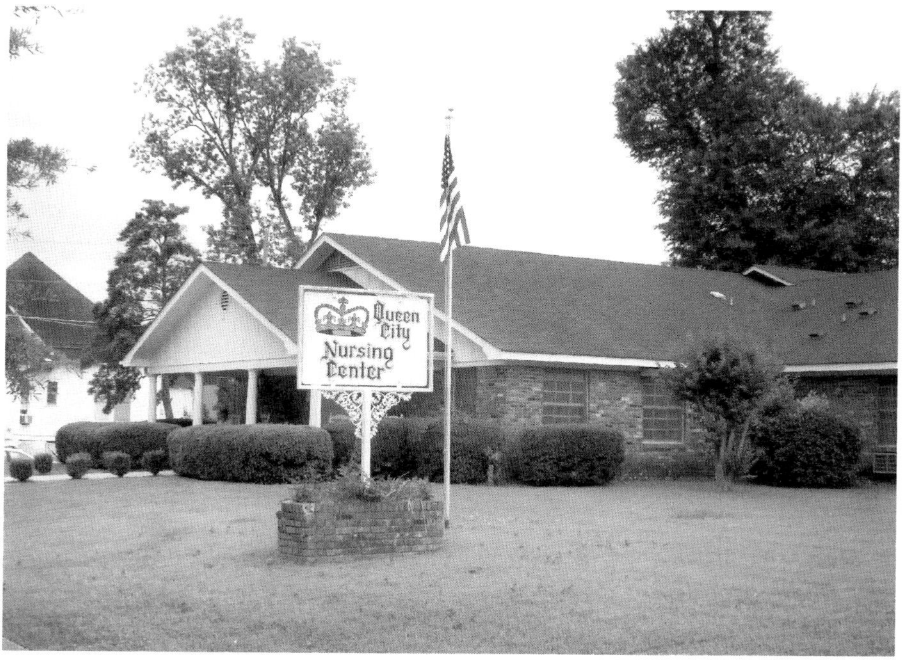

Queen City Nursing Home

the nurse's station, saying, "Get the little boy out! Get the little boy out! And shut the door!" I asked him, "What are you talking about?" I had heard other people mention the ghost, but I had never had a patient lucid enough to talk about it other than to say, "It's kids in the hallway!" He told me that there was a little boy standing behind the door, peeking at him. [Mr. Holland said that] *even as we spoke, the little boy was standing in the corner, watching him and waving his arms. He* [described the boy] *as a little dark-haired kid. Mr. Holland said, "Tell the kid to get out and close the door!"* [I knew] *that telling the kid to get out was not going to help, but I said something* [to the boy] *and closed the door so that the old man would be comfortable. He died a few days later.*

[The next patient to move into the room was Reverend Strong.] *When Reverend Strong got bad, he was saying the same thing. He had gone to the hospital and come here, and the first night that I was there with him, the first thing he said was about the little boy. I said, "Oh, yeah, you better watch him!" Later, the other nurses said, "You're being morbid." We got to talking, and I said, "Remember the last time?" And we started talking about the other patient, Mr. Holland, and it was the*

> *same thing. We talked about the little white boy behind the door. He kept on* [pressing] *the button and trying to get out of bed.* [He'd yell], *"Tell the kid to get out!" And sure enough,* [Reverend Strong] *died two days later. It was real spooky.*
>
> *It had to be the truth because nobody had told Reverend Strong the story about the little boy. So when* [Mr. Holland and Mr. Strong] *had the same manifestations, you've got to* [believe] *there's something to it.*

Ms. Turner was convinced that the Queen City Nursing Home was haunted by the spirit of a child who died in St. Joseph's Hospital. This particular spirit exhibits the characteristics of what paranormal investigators call an "intelligent haunting" because he interacts with the people he is tormenting. The ghost of the little boy is also similar to ghosts like the banshee, whose appearance presages the sudden death of an individual. One can only hope that this little spirit finds rest some day soon—for his sake, and for the sake of the people who see him.

Anderson Regional Medical Center

Today, the Anderson Regional Medical Center is one of Mississippi's largest hospitals. The facility has a staff of seventeen hundred employees, two hundred of whom are staff physicians. However, Anderson Regional Medical Center started out as a two-story wood and brick building, the Turner Infirmary. It was founded in 1910 by Dr. R.I. Turner, who worked at the hospital for seventeen years. Turner Infirmary was small by today's standards, consisting of thirty rooms, an operating room, a laboratory and a surgical department. The hospital closed after Dr. Turner's death in 1927. Then, on March 1, 1928, the building was purchased by Dr. Jeff Anderson. Now known as Anderson Infirmary, Dr. Anderson's hospital had a staff that included three doctors and six nurses and technicians.

In the 1930s, Anderson Infirmary fell upon hard times, as did most of the rest of the nation. To keep the hospital open, Dr. Anderson mortgaged his home on Twenty-third Avenue. Because most of his patients were making barely enough money to live on, Dr. Anderson accepted home-grown vegetables and fruit as payment. Patients who could not afford to pay for their medical care at all were treated for free. Throughout the next decade, a number of improvements were made in Anderson Infirmary during the country's economic recovery. The laboratory was enlarged, and an X-ray department and new operating rooms were added. By 1951, the hospital's medical staff had increased to twenty-four. When Dr. Anderson died that same year, he was replaced by his son, Dr. William Anderson, who immediately changed the name of the hospital to the Jeff Anderson Memorial Hospital.

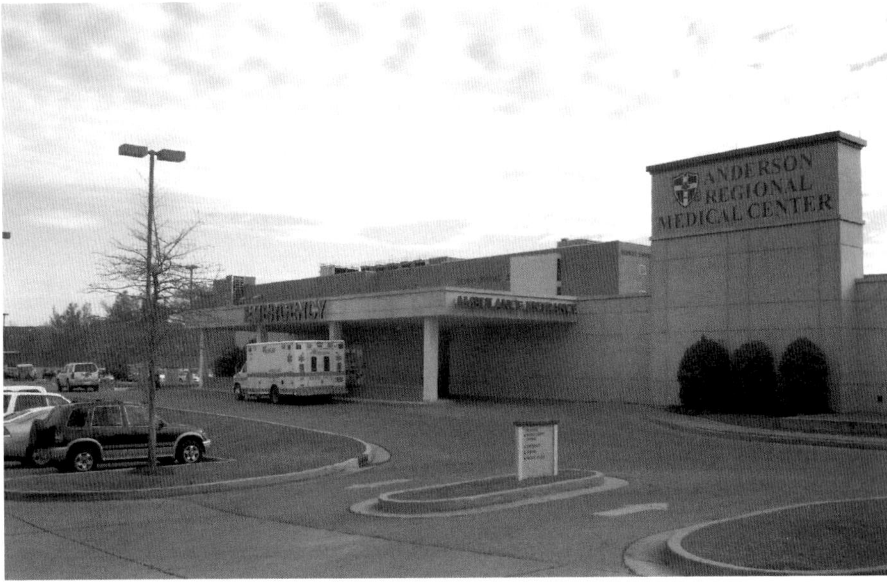

Anderson Regional Medical Center.

In 1955, Dr. William Anderson opened a modernized facility, which included 120 rooms. In addition, several departments, such as X-ray, surgery and obstetrics, were expanded. Jeff Anderson Memorial Hospital experienced another growth spurt twenty years later when the number of private acute-care beds was expanded from 120 to 260. In 1999, Anderson Memorial Hospital offered the region's only open-heart surgery program. The hospital was renamed once again in 2009, becoming Anderson Regional Medical Center to reflect its new services in areas such as women's health, oncology and sleep disorders. On January 1, 2011, the hospital acquired nearby Riley Hospital. Thanks to the purchase, the Anderson Regional Medical Center now has 400 beds and a staff of over seventeen hundred doctors, nurses and technicians. The dedication of one of the nurses in the Labor and Delivery Department seems to have transcended death itself.

One night in 2000, an obstetrics technican named Michelle Hollingsworth was sitting at her desk in the Labor and Delivery Department when she noticed out of the corner of her eye a black woman, dressed as a nurse in a long-sleeved blue gown and scrubs, standing next to her. Thinking that the lady was one of her co-workers, Michelle turned her head to speak to her, but no one was there. "I saw [the ghost] a couple more times on different nights," Michelle said.

> *Finally, I decided I had better ask someone about it. I told one of the nurses, and she said the person I described was actually a nurse who used to work in labor and delivery. One night, the nurse got off work and went home. No one is sure what happened to her, but she was taken back to the hospital, and she died in the ER. Apparently, she had aspirated.*

In 2009, a traveling nurse named Shirley was sitting at the same desk, and she, too, saw the phantom nurse. The nurse walked up to the desk and looked at another nurse, Teresa, who was working at her computer. Assuming that the nurse was looking for someone she knew, Shirley continued writing in her chart. When she looked back up, the nurse was gone.

Nurses are not the only staff members who find it difficult to leave their positions in the department. In 2002, Michelle Hollingsworth was carrying a patient's tray out of Labor Room 3, heading toward the double door. She was walking to the OB hall so that she could put the tray on the food cart. As she passed Room 178, she happened to see an elderly lady with white hair staring out the window toward the parking garage. Her first thought was that the woman was waiting for a family member. Something told the nurse to take another look in the room. When she peered back into Room 178, no one was there. "So I went ahead and took the tray to the OB hall and set it down," Michelle said. "I glanced at a picture on the wall, and suddenly I realized that [the lady in the picture] was the woman who was in that room. She used to be director of nurses for the OB hall from 1946 to 1947."

An OB tech and a nurse had a different sort of paranormal encounter when they were taking a lady to the back of the department to have a C-section. The pair was guiding the stretcher down the hallway when the tech asked the nurse, "Who was that man in black walking down the hallway? He went toward those double doors." The nurse said that she had not seen anyone else in the hallway.

Apparently, labor and delivery is haunted by much younger ghosts as well. Three weeks after Shirley had her sighting, the nursery nurse, as well as two other nurses, heard a baby crying in Labor Room 2. Other nurses have heard the cries of a baby in the hallway.

The ghost of an older child also seems to be haunting the department. Michelle Hollingsworth said that she was working Labor Room 1 all by herself when the temperature dropped significantly. "I could hear a young child whimpering, as if she was hurt," Michelle said.

> *I opened the door and looked down the hallway, and there was nobody there because it was 1:00 or 2:00 in the morning. I heard the little girl crying several other times as well. I was talking to a lady who works in the nursery, and she said that Labor Rooms 1 and 2 in our new department used to be two of the old intensive care rooms. Labor Room 1 is where a little girl between the ages of five and seven passed away many years ago. The nursery nurse told me that the whimpering I was hearing was the sound the little girl made while she was on life support.*

According to paranormal investigators, hospitals are excellent places to find ghosts. Some ghost hunters believe that strong emotion, such as that felt by patients who are in great pain or near death, imprints itself on the walls of buildings. In the case of Anderson Regional Medical Center, at least two of the ghosts that walk its halls are the spirits of former employees who are still carrying out the duties they performed when they were alive. For them, death was not really the end.

Soulé Steam Feed Works

George Wilberforce Soulé was born in Buffalo, New York, in 1849. His family moved to Wisconsin when he was one year old, but when George turned twenty, following his father's death, he left the family farm and embarked on a career as a schoolteacher. In 1875, George moved to Morton, Mississippi. In March 1876, he suffered the loss of his left leg and four toes on his right foot in a railroad accident. Over the next three years, he owned and operated a number of businesses, including a turpentine company, a lumber company and a cotton gin. After moving to Meridian in 1879, George founded the Southern Standard Press Company. By 1881, George had sold 750 cotton presses to cotton gins all over the South.

In 1888, George focused his time and energy on another invention: a small rotary engine that operated on steam. In 1892, he installed one of these small engines in a sawmill. This innovative engine, which was very controllable, enabled the sawyer to feed the carriage through the saw in such a way that the operator could feel his way through the log.

In 1896, Soulé founded the Soulé Steam Feed Works in the Meridian Candy Factory at 402 Nineteenth Avenue. The Meridian Candy Company had been constructed four years earlier. He built an addition to the Meridian Cotton Factory and also constructed a foundry where his workers made the parts for his steam engines. Highly skilled workers created wooden molds of sprockets and gears, which they placed in wooden frames filled with sand. Molten iron was then poured into the void left by the wooden mold. The Soulé Steam Feed Works also manufactured a number of custom-

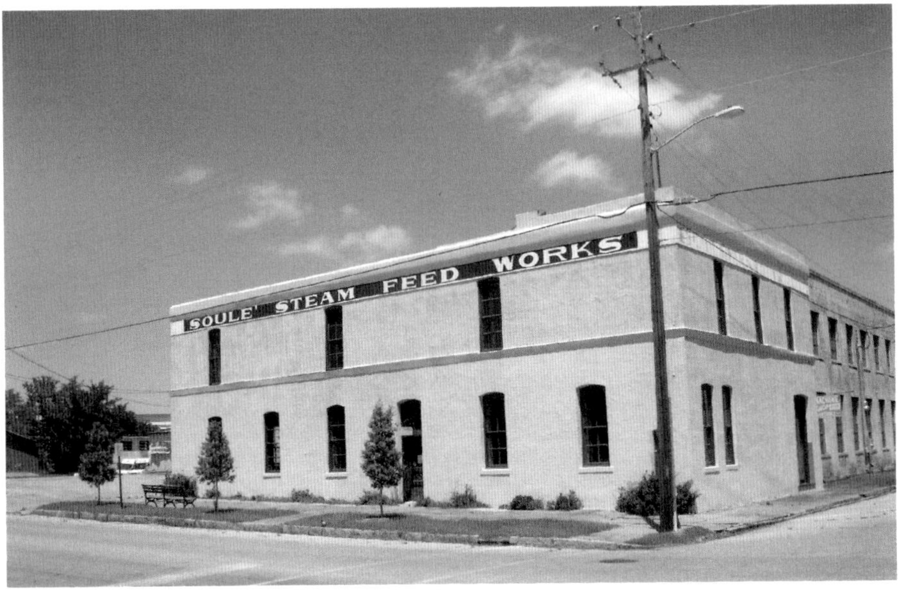

Soulé Steam Feed Works.

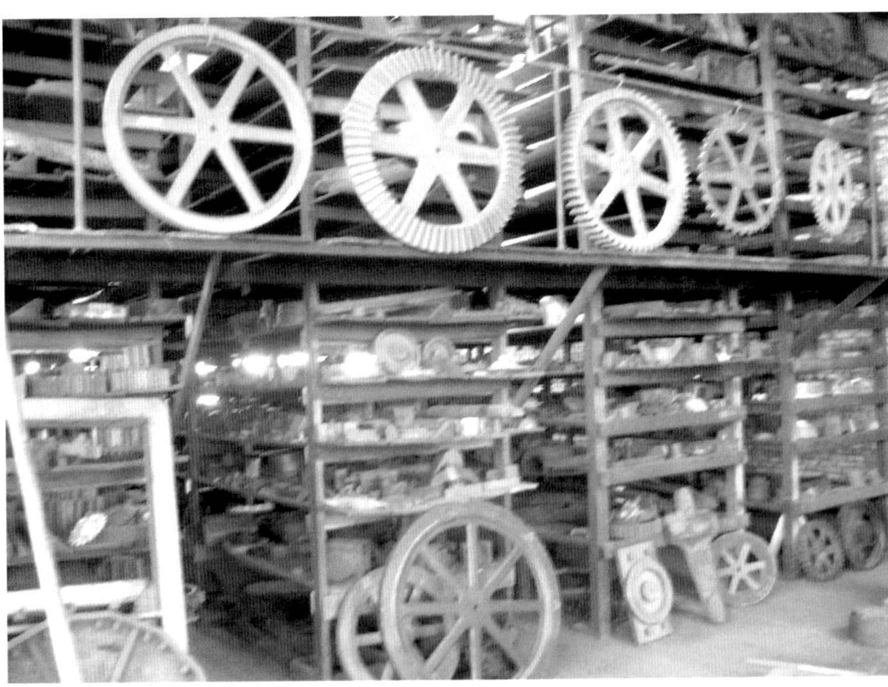

Wooden molds made on-site at the Soulé Steam Feed Works.

made items, such as fireplace implements. One can still find man-hole covers, iron drain grates and the iron ends of benches in Meridian that were made at the Soulé Steam Feed Works.

George Soulé's sons took over operation of the factory after George's death on December 21, 1922. Business peaked in the 1920s, when steam was king. Soulé's steam engines were rolled out into forests across the entire South. As a rule, workers procured water for the engines from streams and ponds. The company's fortunes declined after World War II with the invention of Diesel and electric engines. Soulé Steam Feed Works continued making steam engines for the next three decade, but workers spent most of their time making parts for some of the old engines that were still being used in the South. Soulé produced its last steam engine in 1980, but for some reason, it was never sold. Soulé Steam Feed Works finally closed in 2006, after being in operation for over one hundred years. Soulé's steam engines were so well made that many of them are still being used in South America and India.

In December 1970, the Soulé Steam Feed Works was placed on the National Register of Historic Places as contributing to the Meridian Depot

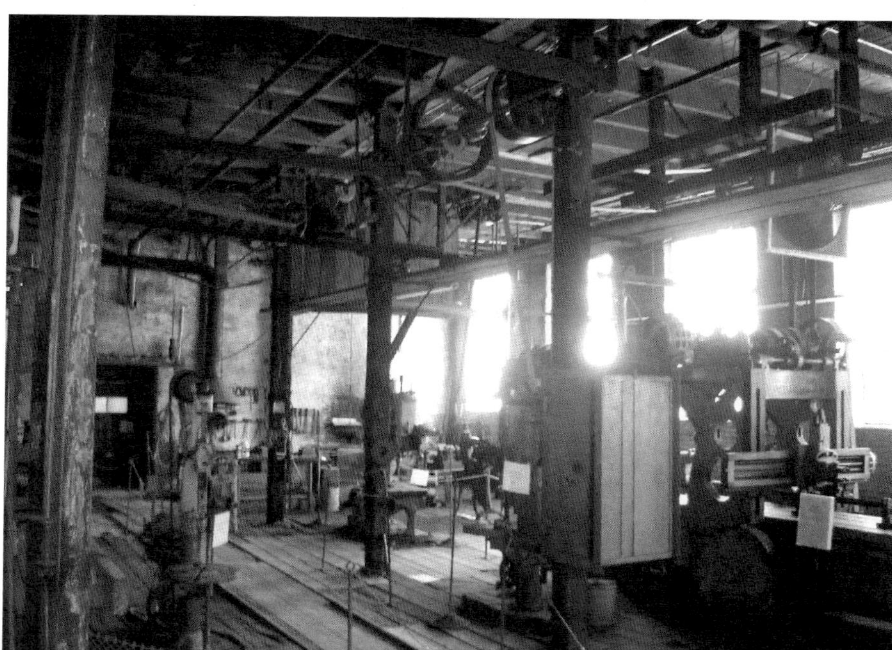

Iron gears and sprockets were transported on these rails from the foundry next door to the main building.

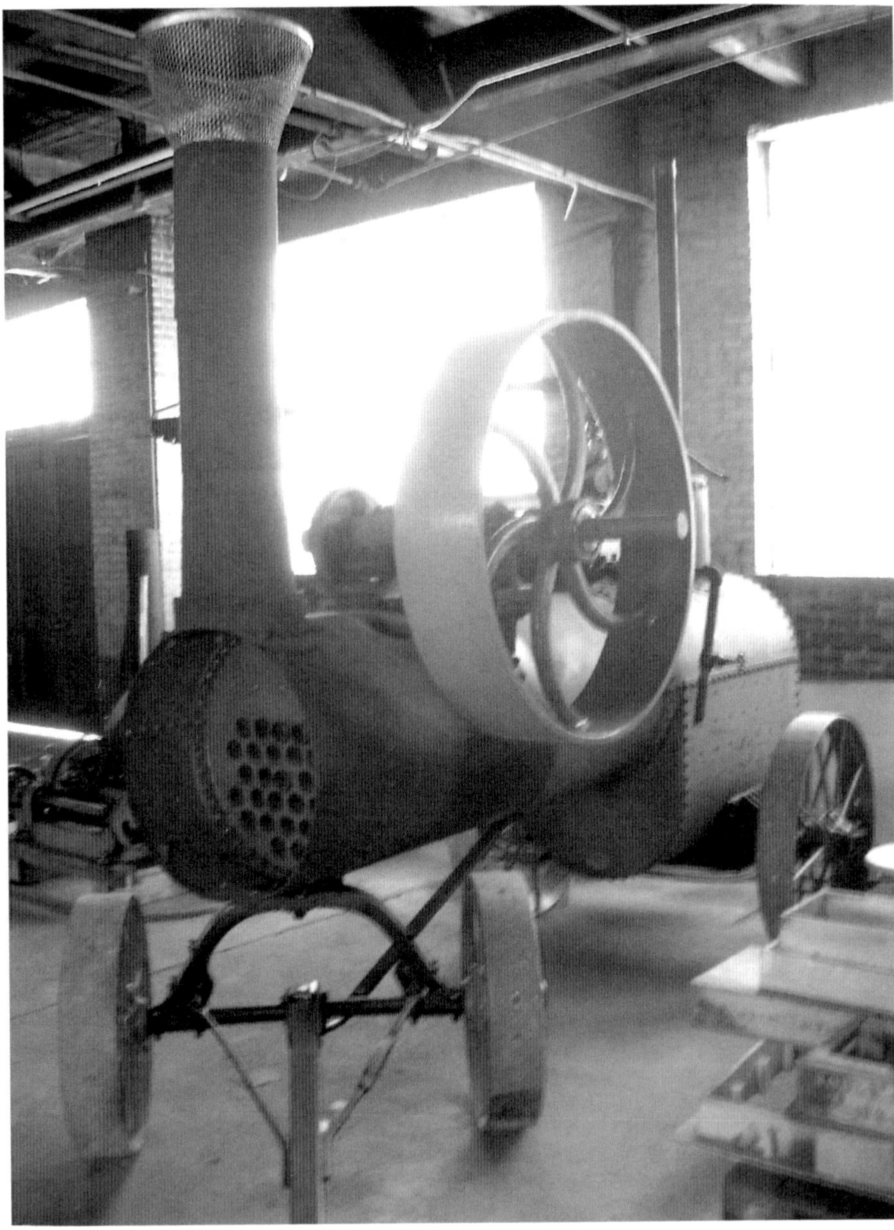

An 1870 steam engine restored by Jim McRae.

Historic District. The building was listed as a Mississippi Historic Landmark in 2003. In 2004, Meridian resident Jim McRae purchased the old factory with the intention of turning it into a museum. When he set about cleaning up the factory, he discovered that it looked almost the same as when his father had taken him there sixty years earlier. Most of the equipment, wooden molds and worktables were still in place on the oil-stained wooden floors. Because Jim enjoys working with old machinery, he refurbished a number of old steam engines, one of which he discovered mired down in a stream in a field. The Soulé Steam Feed Works is so well preserved that walking through the old factory is like stepping back in time. According to one of the museum's workers, part of the building's past is still an active presence.

The ghost that haunts the Soulé Steam Feed Works could be the spirit of the last owner of the old factory, Hal Soulé. Jim McRae remembers Mr. Soulé very well. "Hal was quite a character," Jim said. "He always wore suits with a vest and a tie, even when he walked through the factory. I used to see him quite often at the bank or eating lunch at Weidmann's." Jim clearly remembers one of Hal Soulé's pet peeves: "He was adamant about turning off the lights. He'd walk around the factory in his suit and vest and turn off lights that weren't needed."

In 2002, Meridian resident Greg Hatcher, who had worked in the old factory for eight years, had a very unsettling encounter with Hal Soulé late one evening:

> *I was in the building checking out the records. The Soulés didn't throw away anything, so we still have records pertaining to all of their employees and customers. I had left the lights on in the front of the building and in the vault. As I was getting ready to leave, I said to myself, "I've got to turn the lights off in there." I went in there, and all the lights were turned off. I asked Bob Soulé if he had been in there because he had a key, and there was one other person who had a key—that's me. I asked each person if they had been in the building, and they said no, they hadn't. So I thought that it was really strange that the lights had been cut off. I thought it must have been an electrical problem. Then, the next day, I read that Mr. Hal Soulé had died that afternoon. I said something to some members of the family about it, and they said, "Well, you know, the last thing Hal did before he left Soulé every day was go through behind everybody and turn the lights out." I said, "Well, I guess Mr. Soulé must have gone through and cut out the lights before he left town—permanently." It wasn't really spooky or anything. I just thought that it was a crazy occurrence. It had never happened before or since.*

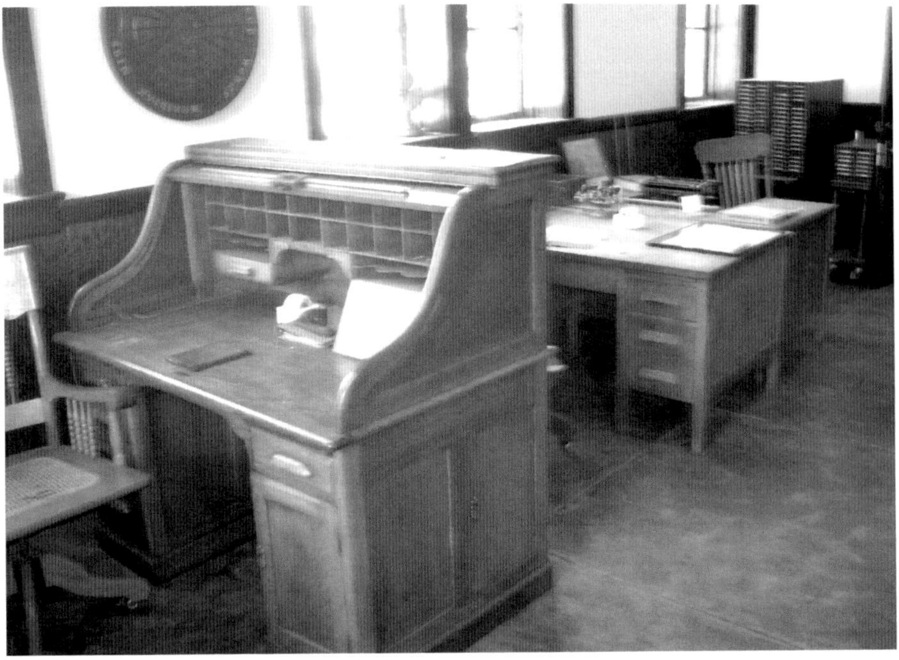

Greg Hatcher was researching records in Mr. Soulé's office when the lights went off.

Today, the Soulé Steam Feed Works operates under a new name: the Mississippi Industrial Heritage Museum, Inc. Each year in November, the museum becomes the centerpiece of the Soulé Steam Festival. Visitors not only view the belt-driven machine shop, the foundry and the steam engine collection, but they also marvel at the "steam show," during which a number of the old steam engines are fired up. The Soulé Steam Feed Works is a reminder that the Old South was much more than cotton fields and antebellum mansions. Factories and foundries, like the Sloss Furnaces in Birmingham, also made invaluable contributions to the economy and the quality of life in the South. The impact that the Soulé family has had on the history of Meridian is still felt today. Some say that one of the Soulés refuses to relinquish control of the family business, even after death.

BIBLIOGRAPHY

Books

Brown, Alan. "Delivering a Few Ghosts." *Weird Encounters*. Edited by Joanne Austin. New York: Sterling Publishing Co., 2010.

———. *Haunted Places in the American South*. Jackson: University Press of Mississippi, 2002.

———. *Shadows and Cypress*. Jackson: University Press of Mississippi, 2000.

———. *Stories from the Haunted South*. Jackson: University Press of Mississippi, 2004.

Fairley, Laura Nan, and James T. Dawson. *Paths to the Past: An Overview History of Lauderdale County, Mississippi*. Meridian, MS: Lauderdale County Department of Archives and History, 1988.

Hubbard, Sylvia Booth. *Ghosts! Personal Accounts of Modern Mississippi Hauntings*. Brandon, MS: Quailridge Press, 1992.

Shank, Jack. *Meridian: The Queen with a Past*. Vol. 1. Meridian, MS: Southeastern Printing Co., 1985.

———. *Meridian: The Queen with a Past*. Vol. 2. Meridian, MS: Southeastern Printing Co., 1986.

———. *Meridian: The Queen with a Past*. Vol. 3. Meridian, MS: Southeastern Printing Co., 1987.

Taylor, Troy. *The Ghost Hunter's Guidebook*. Alton, IL: Whitechapel Productions, 1999.

Weidmann, Mary Dorothy. *The Restaurant: Weidmann's Since 1870*. Booklet, n.d.

PERSONAL INTERVIEWS

Chatham, Kevin. October 2008.
Gullette, Faye. May 20, 2008.
Hooper, Randy. March 17, 2011.
Hoover, Jeannie. December 16, 2006.
Hutcherson, Sheila. August 11, 2010.
Massey, Julia. March 29, 2011.
McCartney, Steven. May 11, 2011.
McLaughlin, Mary. December 15, 2004.
McRae, Jim. April 28, 2011.
Polizzi, Frank. March 17, 2011.
Ramsey, Rhonda. March 29, 2011.
Rigdon, Valarie. March 29, 2011.
Rush, Fonda. November 23, 2010.
Thomas, Steve. July 20, 2010.
Thornton, Dr. Lee K. April 12, 2010.
Todd, Mary K. April 16, 2011.
Turner, Crystal. March 14, 1997.
White, Donna. October 31, 2004.

NEWSPAPERS

Alexander, Ben. "Weidmann's Group Rallies Investors." *Meridian Star*, July 10, 2001.

Bertram, Jack. "Gypsy King, Queen Still Hold Court." *Clarion Ledger*, July 6, 2000.

Brown, Ida. "Ghost Hunters Probe the *Star* for Paranormal Activity." *Meridian Star*, April 24, 2006.

Brown, Jennifer Jacob. "City Working on Downtown Hotel." *Meridian Star*, June 12, 2011.

———. "Elusive 'Lady' Spotted at Grand Opera House." *Meridian Star*, September 15, 2009.

———. "Inside the Threefoot Building." *Meridian Star*, http://meridianstar.com/Local/x46867459/Inside-the-Threefoot-building.

———. "'The Lady' Lingers." *Meridian Star*, October 30, 2009.

———. "The Legendary 'Lady' of the Grand Opera House." *Meridian Star*, October 30, 2007.

———. "Meridian–Lauderdale County Public Library." *Meridian Star*, n.d.

———. "Merrehope: Meridian's Haunted Mansion." *Meridian Star*, n.d.

———. "Queen Kelly Mitchell; A Slice of Meridian's History." *Meridian Star*, December 25, 2007.

———. "Threefoot Building: Endangered Historic Place." *Meridian Star*, May 20, 2010.

Carmichael, Freddie. "Weidmann's: Meridian Landmark in Transition." *Meridian Star*, July 15, 2001.

Cearnal, Sidney. "Boooo! Files Spirited Away by Courthouse Spook." *Meridian Star*, October 27, 1989.

Christian, Maureen. "Jeanne Broach." *Meridian Star*, November 6, 1976.

Dealy, Jessica. "Historic Theater Haunted?" WTOK.com. http://templetheater.wordpress.com.

Fikes, Stephanie. "Ghostly Happenings in Lauderdale County." *Meridian Star*, October 31, 1978.

Horne, Katherine. "Please Don't Take Away the Peanut Butter Crocks." *Meridian Star*, October 30, 2001.

Lockridge, Ben. "Ole Stennis 'Open' House Set for Saturday." *Meridian Star*, December 20, 2006. http://meridianstar.com/business/x681072906/Ole-Stennis-Open-House-set-for-Saturday?k.

McGonagill, Harriet. "Does Old Stagecoach Inn Have Ghosts?" *Meridian Star*, October 30, 1983.

McKey, Anne. "Christmas Time at Merrehope." *Meridian Star*, December 17, 2009. http://meridianstar.com/editorials/x546254893/Christmas-time-at-Merrehope.

Meridian Star. "Jeanne Broach Retires; New Librarian Named." October 2, 1975.

———. "USO Club Occupies A.J. Lyon Residence." January 18, 1942.

Randall, Penny. "Renovations Continue on Weidmann's Square." *Meridian Star*, September 30, 2002.

Smith, Stewart. "Connected to History: Ole Stennis Place Is Still Full of Life." *Meridian Star*, April 2, 2006.

Thompson, Dorothy. "Fundraising Campaign Begins to Repair Historic Williams Home." *Meridian Star*, July 2, 1996.

JOURNALS

"The Parade of Mississippi Enterprise: A Profile of a Successful Firm." *Mississippi Business Review* 11–12 (n.d.).

WEBSITES

Ellisville Mississippi Paranormal Society. "Stuckey's Bridge." http://www.the Ellisvillemississippiparanormalsociety.com/id3.html.

Froehlig, Ada. "Abandoned Stuckey Bridge Road—Mississippi." The Lost Highway. http://www.roadsites.org/losthwy/ms_suckey.html.

Geocaching.com. "Geocaching—The Official GPS Cache Hunt Site." http://www.geocaching.com/seek/cache_details.aspx?guid=30cc8714-f5ff-40e-96bd3-96bd-b28.

Historic Bridges of the U.S. "Stuckey's Bridge." http://bridgehunter.com/ms/hauderdale/stuckeys.

Livingston, Brian. "Experience Creepy with Temple Tour." *Meridian Star.* http://meridianstar.com/local/x921681622/Experience-creepy-with-Temple-tour.

National Register of Historic Places. "Cahn-Crawford House." http://nrhp.focus.nps.gov/natregesearchresult.do?fullresult+true&recordid=1.

National Trust for Historic Preservation. "11 Most Endangered Historic Places: Three-Foot Building." http://www.preservationnation.org/travel-and-sites/sites/southern-region/threefoot-building.

Phil Hardin Foundation. "History and Legacy of the Foundation." http://www.philhardin.org/the-foundation.cfm.

RoadsideAmerica.com. "Meridian, Mississippi—Graves of the King and Queen of the Gypsies." http://www.roadsideakemerica.com/tip/785.

12th Chancery Court District of Mississippi. "Evolution of the Lauderdale County Courthouse." http://chancery12.wordpressl.com/201007/30/evolution-of-the-Lauderdale-county-courthouse.

Vaiden.net. "Rodgers Lineage." http://www.vaiden.net/rodgers_relatives.html.

Wikipedia, s.v. "Meridian City Hall." http://en.wikipedia.org/wiki/Meridian_City_Hall.

———. "Stuckey's Bridge." http://en.wikipedia.org/wiki/Stuckey's_Bridge.

———. "Temple Theater (Meridian, Mississippi)." http://en.wikipedia.org/wiki/Temple_Theater_(Meridian,_Mississippi).

About the Author

Alan Brown was born in Alton, Illinois. After attending Millikin University, Southern Illinois University and the University of Illinois, he taught high school in Springfield, Illinois. In 1986, he began teaching English at the University of West Alabama. After living in the South for a year, Brown became interested in the folklore of the South and began collecting it on his own. "People talk in the Midwest," Brown said, "but not like they do in the South. I guess this is why southerners are great storytellers." When he is not teaching freshman composition or American literature, Dr. Brown writes books on his favorite topic: ghost stories.

As much as he loves old stories that send shivers up the spine, Brown's first love is his wife, Marilyn, his two daughters, Andrea and Vanessa, and his grandson, Cade.